CAMBRIDGE SCHOOL *Chaucer*

THE
Miller's
PROLOGUE AND TALE

Edited by Valerie Allen

CAMBRIDGE
UNIVERSITY PRESS

The publishers would like to thank Professor Helen Cooper for her help in the preparation of this edition.

CAMBRIDGE UNIVERSITY PRESS
Cambridge, New York, Melbourne, Madrid, Cape Town, Singapore, São Paulo

Cambridge University Press
The Edinburgh Building, Cambridge CB2 8RU, UK

www.cambridge.org
Information on this title: www.cambridge.org/9780521701440

First published 2007

Printed in the United Kingdom at the University Press, Cambridge

A catalogue record for this publication is available from the British Library

ISBN 978-0-521-70144-0 paperback

Prepared for publication by Elizabeth Paren
Designed and formatted by Geoffrey Wadsley
Illustrated by Adam Stower
Picture research by Louise Edgeworth

Thanks are due to the following for permission to reproduce photographs:
Alamy, page 13 (Michael Jenner); Ancient Art & Architecture Collection Ltd, pages 14, 82; The
Bridgeman Art Library, pages 23 (Giraudon, Bibliothèque de l'Ecole des Beaux-Arts, Paris, France),
63 (Alinari, Osterreichische Nationalbibliothek, Vienna, Austria), 65 (Lambeth Palace Library, London,
UK), 81 (Bibliothèque Nationale, Paris, France), 84 (Bibliothèque de l'Arsenal, Paris, France); The
British Library, pages 61, 73, 85; Corbis, page 86 (Bernard Bisson/Sygma); Getty Images, page 88
(Hulton Archive); Sonia Halliday, pages 6, 53; TopFoto.co.uk, pages 51 (The British Library/HIP),
92 (Woodmansterne).

For cover photograph: Canterbury Tales: The Miller's Tale, The Art Archive/Eileen Tweedy

Contents

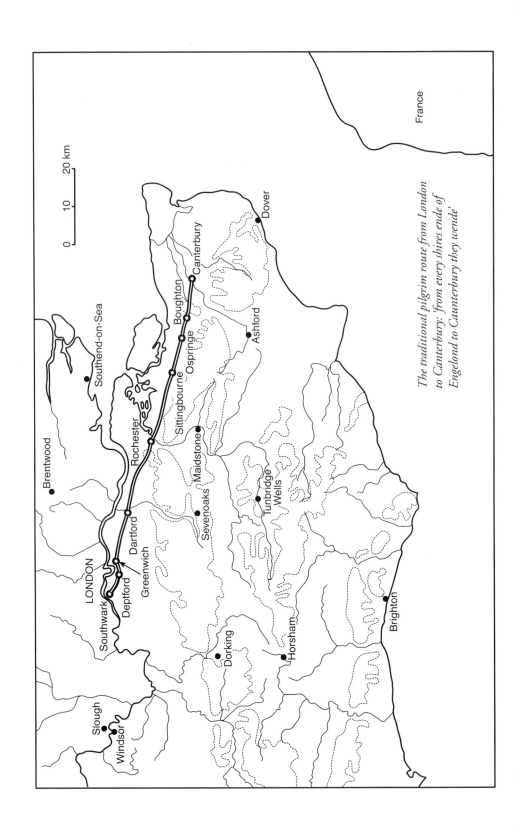

The traditional pilgrim route from London to Canterbury: 'from every shires ende of Engelond to Caunterbury they wende'

Introduction

The first encounter with a page of Chaucer in its original form can be a disconcerting experience. Initially, few words look familiar. Even when the meaning has been puzzled out, the reader is faced with an account of people who lived and died in a world very different from our own. The fourteenth century seems very far away, and you might be forgiven for thinking *The Canterbury Tales* are 'too difficult'.

The aim of this series is, therefore, to introduce you to the world of Chaucer in a way that will make medieval life and language as accessible as possible. With this in mind, we have adopted a layout in which each right-hand page of text is headed by a brief summary of content, and faced by a left-hand page offering a glossary of more difficult words and phrases as well as commentary notes dealing with style, characterisation and other relevant information. There are illustrations, and suggestions for ways in which you might become involved in the text to help make it come alive.

If initial hurdles are lowered, Chaucer's wit and irony, his ability to suggest character and caricature, and his delight in raising provocative and challenging issues from various standpoints, can more readily be appreciated and enjoyed. There is something peculiarly delightful in discovering that someone who lived six hundred years ago had a sense of humour and a grasp of personalities and relationships as fresh and relevant today as it was then.

Each tale provides material for fruitful discussion of fourteenth century attitudes and modern parallels. It is important to realise that the views expressed by the teller of any one tale are not necessarily Chaucer's own. Many of the activities suggested are intended to make you aware of the multiplicity of voices and attitudes in *The Canterbury Tales*. A considerable part of the enjoyment comes from awareness of the tongue-in-cheek presence of the author, who allows his characters to speak for themselves, thereby revealing their weaknesses and obsessions.

Essential information contained in each book includes a brief explanation of what *The Canterbury Tales* are, followed by hints on handling the language. There is then a brief introduction to the teller of the relevant story, his or her portrait from the General Prologue, and an initial investigation into the techniques Chaucer uses to present characters.

The left-hand page commentaries give information applicable to the text. Finally, each book offers a full list of pilgrims, further information on Chaucer's own life and works, some background history, and greater discussion of specific medieval issues. Suggestions for essays are also included. On page 96 is a relatively short glossary of the words most frequently encountered in the text, to supplement the more detailed glossary on each page.

Chaucer's tales are witty, clever and approachable, and raise interesting parallels with life today. His manipulation of the short story form is sophisticated and masterly. We hope this edition will bring *The Canterbury Tales* alive and allow you to appreciate Chaucer's art with ease and enjoyment.

What are *The Canterbury Tales*?

They are a collection of loosely-linked stories, apparently told by a variety of storytellers with very different characters, from different social classes. In fact, both the storytellers themselves and the tales are the creation of one man, Geoffrey Chaucer. Chaucer imagines a group of pilgrims, setting off from the Tabard Inn one spring day to travel from London to St Thomas Becket's shrine in Canterbury – a journey that took about four days.

Canterbury Cathedral window

To make time pass more pleasantly they agree to tell stories to one another. The Host of the Tabard adopts the role of master of ceremonies, and promises a supper at his inn, paid for by the rest of the company, to the one judged to be the best storyteller. Chaucer introduces his pilgrims in descriptions which do much to reveal the character, vices and virtues of each individual. We learn more from the way each person introduces his or her tale, still more from the tales themselves and the way in which each is told, and even further information is offered by the manner in which some pilgrims react to what others say. By this means Chaucer provides a witty, penetrating insight into attitudes, weaknesses, virtues and preoccupations of English men and women of the fourteenth century. At times these may seem very strange to modern readers; at other times they seem just like us.

Linking different tales together by imagining a group of people entertaining one another with storytelling was not a new idea. Boccaccio had famously used a similar notion in the *Decameron*; but he envisaged a group of friends from the same social group, of the same age, with similar interests. Chaucer's pilgrims come from widely differing groups and are very different from one another; they argue, mock, harangue and preach to one another and to us. Just as he depicts them in constant movement, on their unending journey towards Canterbury, so too do they represent the restlessly changing world they inhabited.

THE TALES

Although *The Canterbury Tales* were apparently never completed, enough remains for us to appreciate their richness of texture and ironical comment. The Tales are quite simple - medieval audiences did not expect original plots, but rather clever or unexpected ways of telling stories that might be known in another form. Chaucer's audience of educated friends, witty and urbane courtiers, even, possibly, the king and queen, clearly appreciated his skills. Storytelling was a leisurely process: reading was a social rather than a private activity. Because many people could not read, Chaucer would expect the Tales to be read aloud. If you try to read them like this – you will find advice on pronunciation on page 9 – you will discover they become still more lively and dramatic when spoken.

Most Tales in the collection include aspects of at least one of the following categories, familiar to Chaucer's audience:

Courtly romances These stories of elaborate love affairs were for the upper classes and often told of unrequited love at a distance. The male lover suffered sleepless nights of anguish, wrote poetry, serenaded his beloved with love songs and performed brave feats of noble daring. Meanwhile the beloved (but untouchable) lady sat sewing in her bower, walked in her castle gardens, set her lover impossible tasks, and gave him a scarf or handkerchief as a keepsake. Chaucer pokes gentle fun at this rarefied world view.

Fabliaux Extended jokes or tricks, often bawdy, and commonly full of sexual innuendo. The setting for these was usually contemporary – everyday life in medieval England, peopled by ordinary, flawed human beings. They were as much enjoyed by Chaucer's 'gentil' (or aristocratic) audience as the more restrained romances.

Fables Tales that make a moral point, often using animals as characters.

Sermons Sermons, taking a biblical text as their starting-point, had a moral message. Since 95 per cent of society could not read, sermons had to be good, interesting and full of drama. The line between a good story and a good sermon was very thin indeed. Usually there was an abstract theme (gluttony, avarice, pride) and much use was made of biblical and classical parallels or *exempla* to underline the preacher's point.

Confessions Storytellers sometimes look back over their lives, revealing faults and unhappinesses. This aspect is often introduced in the prologue to the actual story.

The Tales vary widely in content and tone, since medieval stories, Chaucer's included, were supposed both to instruct and entertain. Many have an underlying moral; some, such as the Pardoner's Tale, are also highly dramatic; others, like those told by the Knight and the Squire, have their origins firmly in the courtly love tradition. But many are more complex than this suggests, for the way the tale is told often reflects the disposition and point of view of the teller: although the Nun's Priest's Tale claims to have a moral it hardly justifies the great superstructure of the story; the moral of the Pardoner's Tale is oddly at variance with the immorality of the teller.

The device of using different characters to tell different tales allows Chaucer to distance himself from what is being said, disguising the fact that he controls the varied and opinionated voices of his creations. He pretends, for instance, that he cannot prevent the drunken Miller from telling his vulgar story about the carpenter's wife, and he absolves himself from blame when tellers become sexually explicit. A modern audience may find his frankness and openness about sex surprising, but it was understandable, for there was little privacy, even for the well-to-do, and sexual matters were no secret.

Chaucer's language

The unfamiliar appearance of a page of Chaucerian English prevents many students from pursuing their investigations any further. It does no good telling them that this man used language with a complexity and subtlety not found in any writer of English anywhere before him. They remain unimpressed. He looks incomprehensible.

In fact, with a little help, it does not take very long to master Chaucer's language. Much of the vocabulary is the same as, or at least very similar to, words we use today. On page 96 there is a glossary of unfamiliar words most frequently used in this text, and these will quickly become familiar. Other words and phrases that could cause difficulties are explained on the page facing the actual text.

The language of Chaucer is known as Middle English – a term covering English as it was written and spoken in the period roughly between 1150 and 1500. It is difficult to be more precise than this, for Middle English itself was changing and developing throughout that period towards 'modern' English.

Old English (Anglo-Saxon) was spoken and written until around 1066, the time of the Norman Conquest. This event put power in England into the hands of the Norman lords, who spoke their own brand of Norman French. Inevitably this became the language of the upper classes. The effect was felt in the church, for speedily the control of the monasteries and nunneries was given to members of the new French-speaking aristocracy. Since these religious houses were the seats of learning and centres of literacy, the effect on language was considerable. If you were a wealthy Anglo-Saxon, eager to get on in the world of your new over-lords, you learnt French. Many people were bi- or even trilingual: French was the language of the law courts and much international commerce; Latin was the language of learning (from elementary schools to the highest levels of scholarship) and the church (from parish church services to the great international institution of the papacy).

Gradually, as inter-marriage between Norman French and English families became more common, the distinction between the two groups and the two languages became blurred. Many French words became absorbed into Old English, making it more like the language we speak today. In the thirteenth century King John lost control of his Norman lands, and, as hostility between England and France grew, a sense of English nationalism strengthened. In 1362 the English language was used for the first time in an English parliament. At the same time, Geoffrey Chaucer, a young ex-prisoner of war, was sharpening his pens and his wit, testing the potential for amusement, satire and beauty in this rich, infinitely variable, complex literary tool.

Although two Tales are in prose, *The Canterbury Tales* are written largely in rhyming iambic couplets. This form of regular metre and rhyme is flexible enough to allow Chaucer to write in a range of styles. He uses the couplet form to imitate colloquial speech as easily as philosophical debate. Most importantly, Chaucer wrote poetry 'for the ear': it is written for the listener, as much as for the reader. Rhyme and alliteration add emphasis and link ideas and objects together in a way that is satisfying for the audience. The words jog along as easily and comfortably as the imaginary pilgrims and their horses jogged to Canterbury.

PRONUNCIATION

Chaucer spoke the language of London, of the king's court, but he was well aware of differences in dialect and vocabulary in other parts of the country. In the Reeve's Tale, for instance, he mocks the north country accents of two students. It is clear, therefore, that there were differences in pronunciation in the fourteenth century, just as there are today.

Having said that Chaucer wrote verse to be read aloud, students may be dismayed to find that they do not know how it should sound. There are two encouraging things to bear in mind. The first is that although scholars feel fairly sure they know something about how Middle English sounded, they cannot be certain, and a number of different readings can be heard, so no individual performance can be definitely 'wrong'. The second concerns the strong metrical and rhyming structure Chaucer employed in the writing of his Tales.

Finding the rhythm Follow the rhythm of the verse (iambic pentameter), sounding or omitting the final 'e' syllable in the word as seems most appropriate. In the line
> **And stille he stante under the shot-windowe**

it would add an unnecessary syllable if the final 'e' in 'stille', 'stante' or 'windowe' were pronounced. An 'e' at the end of a word almost always disappears if it is followed by a word beginning with a vowel or an 'h' :
> **He kiste hir sweete and taketh his sautrie**

In the case of the following:
> **This clerk was cleped hende Nicholas.**
> **Of deerne love he koude and of solas;**

the best swing to the regular 10-syllabled line is achieved by sounding the final 'e' (as a neutral vowel sound, like the 'u' in put, or the 'a' in about) in 'hende' and 'deerne', but not in 'koude'.

Other points Where a word begins with the letter 'y' ('yfounde', 'yclad') the 'y' is sounded as it would be in the modern 'party'. Many consonants now silent were pronounced – as in knight, wrong. All the consonants would be given voice in words such as 'neighebores' and 'knokketh' and the 'gh' would be sounded like the Scots 'ch' in 'loch'. The combination 'ow' ('seistow', 'yow') is pronounced as 'how', and the 'ei' in 'seist' would be like the 'a' sound in 'pay'.

For more ideas of what the language might have sounded like, listen to the recording of the Miller's Tale, published by Cambridge University Press.

WARM-UP ACTIVITIES
- Take a section from the Miller's Prologue (lines 12–41 work well) and in a group of four (narrator, Miller, Host and Reeve) read the words aloud, trying to get a sense of the feelings of the speakers.
- Choose a long, self-contained section from the text: lines 147–62 are a useful example. After a brief explanation of the content, if considered necessary, students

work in pairs, speaking alternately, and changing over at each punctuation point. It should be possible to develop a fair turn of speed without losing the sense of the passage.

- Again in pairs choose about ten lines of text; as one of the pair maintains a steady beat (^/^/^/^/^/) the partner does his or her best to fit the words to the rhythm.
- Choose a long self-contained unit from the text. Students walk round the room, speaking the script, and turning left or right at each punctuation mark. The carpenter's 'rescue' of Nicholas (lines 340–63) is a good example of a speech that gives ample opportunity for a splendidly melodramatic interpretation, as do lines 405–25. The Miller's Tale is one of the liveliest tales and maximum enjoyment can be obtained from dramatic presentation.

GRAMMATICAL POINTS

Emphatic negatives Whereas a person who stated that he 'wasn't going nowhere, not never' might be considered grammatically incorrect nowadays, Chaucer uses double or triple negatives quite often, to give a statement powerful added emphasis. One of the best known is in his description of the Knight:

> **He never yet no vilenye ne sayde**
> **In al his life, unto no manner wight.**

This emphasis frequently occurs in the Miller's Tale, in lines such as:

> **In al the toun nas brewhous ne taverne**
> **That he ne visited with his solas,**

In both cases the multiple negatives strengthen the force of what is being said.

Word elision In modern written English words and phrases are often run together (elided) to represent the spoken form of those words: 'didn't', 'can't', 'won't', 'I've' and so on. Chaucer uses short forms of words too, usually when a character is speaking, and most frequently when he is using the word 'thou' (you). Examples include the following:

> **willtow** – will you **hastow** – have you
> **woostow** – do you know

The 'y' prefix The past participle of a verb sometimes has a 'y' before the rest of the verb:

> **he was in a marle-pit yfalle** he had fallen in a clay-pit
> **fetisly ydight with herbes swoote** pleasantly decorated with sweet herbs

The 'possessive' form of nouns In modern English we indicate possession by means of an apostrophe: 'the hat of the man' becomes 'the man's hat'. Middle English had a particular formation that is still used in modern German – where we now use an apostrophe followed by an 's', Chaucer uses the suffix 'es'. So 'the man's hat' becomes 'the mannes hat' – the second 'n' indicating that the word has two syllables.

The Miller's contribution

The list of Canterbury pilgrims in the General Prologue not only indicates character and appearance but also status. By beginning with the Knight and his retinue, and ending with rogues and cheats (such as the Miller and the Reeve) Chaucer shows how important order of precedence was in medieval society. This list can be found on page 85.

The storytelling competition devised by Harry Baily, the Host, is intended to proceed in an orderly fashion, higher-ranking pilgrims speaking first. The Knight's courtly, romantic tale (see page 82) is well received by all; the Monk is invited to speak next. But this stately, conventional procedure is emphatically disrupted by the Miller's intervention, followed by the Reeve's. The ideal of ordered society, in which people know their place and stick to it, is shattered by the vociferous vigour of the lower classes. Any attempt to impose such a rigid pattern is questioned by the very shape of *The Canterbury Tales* themselves.

The Miller tells a vulgar, amoral and funny parody of the Knight's tale. Chaucer pretends that events and characters are beyond his control, and that this interruption is none of his doing, but by juxtaposing noble Knight and common Miller, and by allowing later pilgrims to argue, disagree and interrupt one another, he achieves an exuberant blend of styles, attitudes and material. All responses and points of view are open to question, by other pilgrims as well as the wider audience. Readers are invited to judge for themselves, and to see how each story reflects the disposition of the teller.

The Miller's Tale offers a riposte to the idealistic Knight's opening story; it also indicates to Chaucer's wider audience that in the world of the late fourteenth century the voice of a drunken Miller resounds as forcefully as a nobleman's. Social attitudes changed in the economic disruption following the Black Death. In 1381 Wat Tyler's peasant army marched from Canterbury to London demanding that the king heard their grievances. Chaucer's original audience would have noted the significance of the Miller's forceful intervention.

In the General Prologue Robin the Miller is an ugly customer, who wins prizes for brawling, and removes doors from their hinges by headbutting them. He swears he can 'quite' (perform as well as) the Knight with his 'noble' story. In fact it is markedly different in tone, structure and language from the Knight's tale. The storytelling competition comes to life as the Miller offers his slant on questions raised by the Knight. Similar themes recur in later tales: marriage; women in society; religion and superstition; friction between workmen and students. By using many different storytellers Chaucer adds immeasurably to the texture of his work, manipulating tales, tellers, attitudes and arguments, denying responsibility for what is said, and concealing his own point of view. Chaucer insists it is all a game, thus releasing himself from the need for serious moral guidelines. Unsettling aspects of the changing world around him find voice in characters and stories. The position and content of the Miller's Tale sets the tone for the unresolved questions that concerned Chaucer's original audience and still engage us today.

In Chaucer's description of the Miller in the General Prologue much of the Miller's character is revealed through his unpleasant physical appearance. Millers were powerful members of any community, and had a reputation for dishonesty and sharp practice.

- Discuss the way Chaucer deliberately emphasises certain aspects of the Miller's character here, through simile, tone and vocabulary. Using evidence obtained from the activities with which he is associated, and the way in which he is described, draw up a list of the Miller's main characteristics. You may wish to read some of the passage aloud, noting how often sound reinforces sense. If you prefer, make a drawing of the Miller, labelling your key points.
- Every community needed a miller to grind the corn from all the neighbouring fields. What, if any, information are you given here about this Miller's trade?
- Why is this man on a pilgrimage? See pages 87–88 for information about pilgrimages.
- Write a description of someone from the 21st century similar to the Miller; use Chaucer's method of building his character from small details of appearance and behaviour. You may wish to write in iambic pentameter.

547–8	**stout carl ... eek of bones** a very well-built ruffian indeed, brawny and thick-boned too		561	**greet forneys** huge furnace
549	**over al ther he cam** above all others, wherever he went		562	**janglere and a goliardeys** loudmouth and teller of crude stories
550	**the ram** the traditional prize for wrestling		563	**moost of sinne and harlotries** usually about sin and sexual exploits
551	**short-sholdred ... knarre** short-necked, broad, a thickset fellow		564	**tollen thries** take three times his rightful portion for grinding the corn
552	**no dore ... harre** no door he was unable to heave off its hinges		565	**a thombe of gold, pardee** by God he had a golden thumb [Millers used their thumbs to judge the quality of the corn they ground; a good judge (or maybe a dishonest miller) would be a rich one.]
553	**at a renning** by running at it			
554	**reed** red [Red hair traditionally denotes fiery temper.]			
556	**cop** top			
557	**werte** wart			
558	**the brustles of a sowes eris** the bristles in a sow's ears		567	**baggepipe** a noisy instrument, typical of the countryside, sometimes played by devils in medieval illustrations
559	**nosethirles** nostrils			

The description of the Miller in the General Prologue.

The Millere was a stout carl for the nones;
Ful big he was of brawn, and eek of bones.
That proved wel, for over al ther he cam,
At wrastlinge he wolde have alwey the ram.   550
He was short-sholdred, brood, a thikke knarre;
Ther was no dore that he nolde heve of harre,
Or breke it at a renning with his heed.
His berd as any sowe or fox was reed,
And therto brood, as though it were a spade.   555
Upon the cop right of his nose he hade
A werte, and theron stood a toft of heris,
Reed as the brustles of a sowis eris;
His nosethirles blake were and wide.
A swerd and bokeler bar he by his side.   560
His mouth as greet was as a greet forneys.
He was a janglere and a goliardeys,
And that was moost of sinne and harlotries.
Wel koude he stelen corn and tollen thries;
And yet he hadde a thombe of golde, pardee.   565
A whit cote and a blew hood wered he.
A baggepipe wel koude he blowe and sowne,
And therwithal he broghte us out of towne.

'A baggepipe wel koude he blowe and sowne'

13

Until now everything has gone according to the Host's plan for a storytelling game. The Knight (by luck or clever management on the Host's part) told the first, appropriately 'noble', story, particularly enjoyed by the 'gentil' folk. According to rules governing social etiquette the Monk, as highest-ranking churchman, should speak next. But, apparently upsetting a convention which had been adhered to quite closely in the General Prologue, the Miller, clearly a rogue, and almost at the end of that introductory list of pilgrims, riotously disrupts the orderly procedure. See note on the Miller's contribution on page 11.

- Working in a group, discuss how other pilgrims might have reacted to the events described in these lines (for example, the Knight and his son, the Squire, or the ladylike Prioress, the Monk or the Friar). You could give a dramatic presentation, illustrating the contrast between the Host's behaviour, as Master of Ceremonies, and that of the Miller.

- Discuss with a partner how Chaucer emphasises the difference in status between Knight and Miller in lines 1–24. Make a list of the aspects of the Miller's behaviour which already label him as common and ignoble.

2–3	**nas ther ... storie** neither young nor old could deny it was a noble story
5	**namely ... everichon** particularly all the well-bred people
6	**so moot I gon** as I live and prosper
7	**unbokeled is the male** the bag is opened [the game has begun]

'he was dronke of ale'

11	**to quite with** to equal, or pay back [requite]
12	**for dronken ... pale** pale with drunkenness
13	**unnethe** could scarcely
14	**nolde avalen ... ne hat** would not remove hood nor hat as a courtesy to anyone
16	**Pilates vois** Pilate's voice [In the Mystery Plays Pilate was traditionally played as a ranting tyrant.]
17	**By armes, and by blood and bones** a violent, irreverent oath, referring to Christ's body
18	**I kan ... for the nones** I know a noble tale for the occasion [We already suspect it will be far from noble.]
21	**Abyd ... brother** wait, dear brother [or good friend] Robin
23	**werken thriftily** do things in an appropriate manner
25	**go my wey** go off on my own
26	**a devel wey** in the devil's name

All the pilgrims admired the Knight's tale, and the Host invites the Monk to tell something equally entertaining. However, the drunken Miller interrupts, insisting he will speak next.

Whan that the Knight had thus his tale ytoold,
In al the route nas ther yong ne oold
That he ne seide it was a noble storie,
And worthy for to drawen to memorie;
And namely the gentils everichon. 5
Oure Hooste lough and swoor, 'So moot I gon,
This gooth aright; unbokeled is the male.
Lat se now who shal telle another tale;
For trewely the game is wel bigonne.
Now telleth ye, sir Monk, if that ye konne 10
Somwhat to quite with the Knightes tale.'
   The Millere, that for dronken was al pale,
So that unnethe upon his hors he sat,
He nolde avalen neither hood ne hat,
Ne abide no man for his curteisie, 15
But in Pilates vois he gan to crie,
And swoor, 'By armes, and by blood and bones,
I kan a noble tale for the nones,
With which I wol now quite the Knightes tale'.
   Oure Hooste saugh that he was dronke of ale, 20
And seide, 'Abyd, Robin, my leeve brother;
Som bettre man shal telle us first, another.
Abyd, and lat us werken thriftily.'
   'By Goddes soule,' quod he, 'that wol nat I;
For I wol speke, or elles go my wey.' 25
   Oure Hooste answerde, 'Tel on, a devel wey!
Thou art a fool; thy wit is overcome.'

The disagreement between the Reeve and the Miller begins before the Miller has even started to tell his story. Certainly a reeve, as an estate-manager, would feel deep-rooted suspicions towards a cheating miller; but their antipathy seems more personal than this.

- Look carefully at the exchange between Reeve and Miller printed opposite and see how their mutual dislike is revealed, and how much you can discover about the characters of both men and the possible reasons for their enmity. It will help to know that the Reeve is also a carpenter by trade.

- It seems very likely that Chaucer planned that his *Canterbury Tales* should begin with the Knight's, Miller's and Reeve's tales following one another – even though he pretends not to be responsible. When you have finished reading this tale look again at these early pages, and discuss why he may have made this decision.

28	**alle and some** all of you
30	**soun** sound
31	**if that I misspeke or seye** if I speak or say anything improper
32	**wite it** put it down to, blame it on
33	**legende** story [usually used of bible stories]
35	**how that a clerk hath set the wrightes cappe** how a university student made a fool of the carpenter
36	**stint thy clappe** shut your mouth
37	**lat be** leave off
	harlotrie filthy talk
39	**apeyren** victimise
40–1	**eek to bringen ... thinges seyn** and also to speak so slanderously about wives. You can say plenty about other matters. [The question of whether a 'good wife' can be found will appear in many other tales.]
44	**Who hath ... cokewold** only the man without a wife is never a cuckold [deceived husband]

47	**ayeyns** against
48	**but if thou madde** unless you're insane
51	**nolde I** I would not wish [negative form of 'wolde']
52–3	**Take upon me ... that I were oon** assume too much as to whether I might be one [a cuckold]
55–8	**An housbonde ... nedeth nat enquere** A husband shouldn't look too closely into God's secrets, or his wife's. As long as he has sufficient of God's bounty for himself, there's no reason to look too closely for the rest. [This theme of being content to accept God's divine purpose without too much questioning recurs more than once in this tale, purportedly told by a simple man uninterested in philosophy or theological questioning. In these lines the Miller seems to suggest that God and women are both a mystery to an honest fellow.]

The Miller blames the crudeness of his tale on the Southwark ale he's drunk. The Reeve objects to a
story about wives, which he fears may be insulting; the Miller replies that lots of wives are faithful
(i.e. some aren't) – and husbands should not pry too closely into their wives' secrets.

'Now herkneth,' quod the Millere, 'alle and some!
But first I make a protestacioun
That I am dronke, I knowe it by my soun;   30
And therfore if that I misspeke or seye,
Wite it the ale of Southwerk, I you preye.
For I wol telle a legende and a lyf
Bothe of a carpenter and of his wyf,
How that a clerk hath set the wrightes cappe.'   35
    The Reve answerde and seide, 'Stint thy clappe!
Lat be thy lewed dronken harlotrie.
It is a sinne and eek a greet folie
To apeyren any man, or him defame,
And eek to bringen wives in swich fame.   40
Thou mayst ynogh of othere thinges seyn.'
    This dronke Millere spak ful soone ageyn
And seide, 'Leve brother Osewold,
Who hath no wyf, he is no cokewold.
But I sey nat therfore that thou art oon;   45
Ther been ful goode wives many oon,
And evere a thousand goode ayeyns oon badde.
That knowestow wel thyself, but if thou madde.
Why artow angry with my tale now?
I have a wyf, pardee, as wel as thow;   50
Yet nolde I, for the oxen in my plogh,
Take upon me moore than ynogh,
As demen of myself that I were oon;
I wol bileve wel that I am noon.
An housbonde shal nat been inquisitif   55
Of Goddes privetee, nor of his wyf.
So he may finde Goddes foison there,
Of the remenant nedeth nat enquere.'

The Miller's Tale was most likely written after many of the other *Canterbury Tales*, and chosen to fit precisely where it comes in the sequence – after the Knight's Tale and before the Reeve's Tale. Chaucer's pretence that the voice of this common lout is an unstoppable interruption is in fact part of the careful design that embraces *The Canterbury Tales* in their entirety.

• As the tale progresses, make a note of examples of the Miller's influence on what is told and the language used.

• Consider whose 'voice' you hear in lines 59–78. Is it Chaucer the poet or Chaucer the pilgrim and reporter of the journey to Canterbury? What would you expect the likely differences to be between a story told by a Knight and that told by a Miller? (You might find it helpful to read the description of the Knight on page 17 in the General Prologue, before you answer.)

60	**nolde his wordes for no man forbere** would not stop talking for anyone [The double negative 'nolde' – 'no man' – emphasises the Miller's determination to speak and the author's determination to take no responsibility for his character's tale.]
61	**cherles tale** a low story – told by a churl, the lowest social class in medieval England. [In fact the story is a fabliau – popular with all classes. See page 7 for further details.]
62	**M'athinketh that ... heere** it pains me that I must repeat it here [Not true, of course, Chaucer and his audience enjoyed a good bawdy story.]
64–5	**demeth nat that I ... ivel intente** don't think that I speak with evil intent
65	**moot reherce** must repeat
67	**elles falsen som of my mateere** or else falsify my reported account
68–9	**whoso list it ... chese another tale** whoever doesn't want to hear it, let him turn the page and choose another tale [The author is fully aware that this tale has a far wider reading audience than the fictional pilgrims who listen to it on their way to Canterbury.]
71–2	**gentillesse ... hoolinesse** true nobility, and also moral lessons and saintly behaviour
73	**chese amis** choose wrongly
75	**othere mo** others too
76	**harlotrie** crude and uncouth stories
77	**aviseth yow** be warned
78	**eek men shal nat maken ernest of game** don't take a game too seriously [Chaucer reminds his audience that the tales are supposedly a light-hearted competition designed to make the journey to Canterbury pass speedily.]

Chaucer says he will re-tell the tale in the Miller's own words, and therefore begs 'gentlefolk' not to take offence. If they don't wish to hear it they should choose another story – for there are plenty to choose from.

What sholde I moore seyn, but this Millere
He nolde his wordes for no man forbere,   60
But tolde his cherles tale in his manere.
M'athinketh that I shal reherce it heere.
And therfore every gentil wight I preye,
For Goddes love, demeth nat that I seye
Of ivel entente, but for I moot reherce   65
Hir tales alle, be they bettre or werse,
Or elles falsen som of my mateere.
And therfore, whoso list it nat yheere,
Turne over the leef and chese another tale;
For he shal finde ynowe, grete and smale,   70
Of storial thing that toucheth gentillesse,
And eek moralitee and hoolinesse.
Blameth nat me if that ye chese amis.
The Millere is a cherl, ye knowe wel this;
So was the Reve eek and othere mo,   75
And harlotrie they tolden bothe two.
Aviseth yow, and put me out of blame;
And eek men shal nat maken ernest of game.

- We are given very little information about the carpenter here, but a vivid impression of Nicholas is carefully built up from factual details. Much of what we are told is concerned with outward impressions. Does he seem 'poor'? Is this picture entirely favourable? Compare this description with the Clerk of Oxenforde from the General Prologue.
- 'Hende' is an adjective so frequently applied to Nicholas that the reader quickly suspects it is used ironically. Make a note of when and where it appears in the tale. How much of what we learn about Nicholas, even at this early stage, is purely superficial, suggesting there may be hidden aspects to his character?
- Chaucer stresses that the carpenter is a 'gnof' (a word to be spoken aloud for full effect). What would you expect his reaction to be towards his lodger? You might need to revise this initial response after reading the story.
- Although his reputation as an astrologer will prove to be important, the account of Nicholas' astrological skills is deliberately vague; he seems able to forecast weather and predict the future. See page 93 for an account of astrology and astronomy in the fourteenth century.

79	**whilom** once upon a time	
80	**riche gnof** wealthy lout [you can be rich, but still low]	
	gestes heeld to bord rented rooms to lodgers	
82	**poure scoler** impoverished student	
83	**hadde lerned art** had studied the university curriculum in arts [grammar, logic, rhetoric: the trivium]	
84	**fantasie ... astrologie** passion was directed to studying astrology [Merton College was a centre for this.]	
85–90	**And koude a certein ... rekene hem alle** And he knew some practical experiments by which he could work out through his enquiries at what particular time men might expect drought or showery weather, furthermore, if asked, he could predict the outcome in any sort of situation – I can't tell all his talents	
91	**hende** an all-embracing term of approval – near at hand, but also polite, clean, tidy, clever, helpful – nice [The word is used ironically and frequently about Nicholas, who turns out to be anything but nice.]	
92	**deerne love ... solas** he knew plenty about secret love affairs and such games	
93	**sleigh ... privee** sly and very secretive	
94	**lyk a maiden ... for to see** outwardly modest as a girl	
97	**fetisly ydight** pleasantly decorated	
98–9	**as sweete ... cetewale** fresh as liquorice or ginger root	
100	**Almageste** Ptolemy's work on astrology [widely used in Chaucer's time]	
101	**astrelabie** astrolabe – astronomical instrument	
	longinge for belonging to	
102	**augrim stones** counting stones [used with an abacus]	
	layen faire apart carefully set out	
104	**falding reed** coarse red cloth	

John, a wealthy Oxford carpenter, rents a room in his house to a poor scholar, Nicholas, passionately interested in astrology and secret love affairs. He and his room are delightfully and carefully presented.

Whilom ther was dwellinge at Oxenford
A riche gnof, that gestes heeld to bord,   80
And of his craft he was a carpenter.
With him ther was dwellinge a poure scoler,
Hadde lerned art, but al his fantasie
Was turned for to lerne astrologie,
And koude a certein of conclusiouns,   85
To demen by interrogaciouns,
If that men asked him in certein houres
Whan that men sholde have droghte or elles shoures,
Or if men asked him what sholde bifalle
Of every thing; I may nat rekene hem alle.   90
This clerk was cleped hende Nicholas.
Of deerne love he koude and of solas;
And therto he was sleigh and ful privee,
And lyk a maiden meke for to see.
A chambre hadde he in that hostelrie   95
Allone, withouten any compaignie,
Ful fetisly ydight with herbes swoote;
And he himself as sweete as is the roote
Of licoris, or any cetewale.
His Almageste, and bookes grete and smale,   100
His astrelabie, longinge for his art,
His augrim stones, layen faire apart
On shelves couched at his beddes heed;
His presse ycovered with a falding reed;

- Music played an important part in fourteenth-century life. Those who could play and sing well were always popular members of society. Young Nicholas with his 'sautrie' and his fine voice would have been much in demand. Start to make notes on when and where singing and music-making are referred to in this tale, and how they are important.
- The theme of old husband and frivolous young wife recurs in many of the tales. Marrying for love was less common than marrying for financial gain, or the need to produce heirs. As this tale progresses, decide whether Chaucer reveals either sympathy for his characters or moral disapproval.

105 **gay sautrie** merry psaltery [A flattish, wooden stringed instrument, similar to a dulcimer, but plucked with fingernails or plectrum, with a light, cheerful sound – more refined than the Miller's uncouth bagpipes.]

108 ***Angelus ad virginem*** *The angel appeared to the virgin* – a hymn, with a very jolly tune, on the annunciation [Nicholas will confront this carpenter's wife in similar manner to the angel, but with rather different intentions.]

109 **Kinges Noote** another [unidentified] song

110 **ful often ... mirie throte** he was often heard joyfully singing [possibly he found it profitable]

112 **after his freendes finding and his rente** living on the generosity of friends and his own income

116 **heeld hire narwe in cage** kept her most closely confined

118 **demed himself ... a cokewold** considered himself likely to be cuckolded

119–20 **He knew nat ... similitude** because he was ignorant he didn't know Cato's advice that a man should marry someone of similar age and status. [Chaucer frequently refers to a collection of pithy wise sayings, attributed to the Latin poet, Cato, and well known to literate men – but not to millers.]

121 **after hire estaat** like themselves

122 **at debaat** in conflict

123 **sith that** since

snare the trap [of taking a young wife]

124 **he moste endure ... his care** he had to put up with his trouble, as other folk do

Nicholas passes his evenings playing the psaltery and singing, living off money given by friends and his own income. The old carpenter has a beautiful, headstrong young wife, Alison, whom he guards jealously, fearful that she might be unfaithful.

And al above ther lay a gay sautrie,   105
On which he mad a-nightes melodie
So swetely that all the chambre rong;
And *Angelus ad virginem* he song;
And after that he song the Kinges Noote.
Ful often blessed was his mirie throte.   110
And thus this sweete clerk his time spente
After his freendes finding and his rente.
   This carpenter hadde wedded newe a wyf,
Which that he lovede moore than his lyf;
Of eighteteene yeer she was of age.   115
Jalous he was, and heeld hire narwe in cage,
For she was wilde and yong, and he was old,
And demed himself been lik a cokewold.
He knew nat Catoun, for his wit was rude,
That bad man sholde wedde his similitude.   120
Men sholde wedden after hire estaat,
For youthe and elde is often at debaat.
But sith that he was fallen in the snare,
He moste endure, as oother folk, his care.

'This carpenter hadde wedded newe a wyf, Which that he lovede moore than his lyf'

- The description of the carpenter's wife is one of the great set pieces of this tale – indeed of the Tales as a whole. Spend time analysing the information we are given here. It was a convention of romantic storytelling that the beauty of the heroine should be described in minute detail – but this description is subtly different from the conventional mode (see page 84). The comparison with the weasel, for example, certainly suggests her graceful figure, but a weasel might be associated with other, less pleasant characteristics. Which other comparisons in these lines do you find to be similarly ambivalent?
- Using similar techniques to Chaucer's own, write a description of a young woman of today, who, like the carpenter's wife, is devastatingly attractive, but definitely not a lady. Use a similar verse form too, if you wish.
- What, to you, seems to be Chaucer's attitude towards this woman? Support your answer with details from these lines.

125	**therwithal** in addition	136	**sikerly ... eye** truly she had a seductive expression [Chaucer hardly needs to tell us this.]
126	**wezele** weasel		
	gent and smal supple and slight	137	**smale ypulled** finely plucked [Plucked eyebrows were considered sinful.]
127	**ceint ... of silk** she wore a striped girdle of silk [Her clothes are unusually fine for a carpenter's wife.]		
		138	**sloo** sloe berry
128–9	**barmcloth ... many a goore** apron, white as morning milk, and lavishly pleated, around her hips [clearly for show, not housework]	139–41	**ful moore blisful ... a wether** she was far more beautiful to see than a newly blossoming sweet pear tree, softer to touch than the wool of a young wether, or female sheep [He's telling us she's at the peak of her natural beauty, and inviting us to poke her.]
130	**smok** shift, underdress [Her clothes are chosen to show off her own dramatic colouring and slim figure.]		
130–2	**broiden ... withoute** embroidered back and front, inside and out, with coal-black silk round the collar	143	**perled with latoun** decorated with showy brass studs
133	**voluper** head-dress or kerchief [with fastening tapes similarly embroidered]	144–6	**in al this ... or swich a wenche** in all the world, even if he looked everywhere, there would not be a man who could possibly imagine or discover such a lively sweetheart or such a girl [The double negative 'nis no' adds emphasis to an already forceful statement – and the word 'wenche' is only used to describe women from the lower classes.]
135	**filet brood** broad head-band [deliberately set high to draw attention to her eyes and eyebrows]		

The young wife's looks, dress and demeanour are vividly described, in these lines and overleaf.

Fair was this yonge wyf, and therwithal   125
As any wezele hir body gent and smal.
A ceint she werede, barred al of silk,
A barmclooth eek as whit as morne milk
Upon hir lendes, ful of many a goore.
Whit was hir smok, and broiden al bifoore   130
And eek bihinde, on hir coler aboute,
Of col-blak silk, withinne and eek withoute.
The tapes of hir white voluper
Were of the same suite of hir coler;
Hir filet brood of silk, and set ful hye.   135
And sikerly she hadde a likerous ye;
Ful smale ypulled were hire browes two,
And tho were bent and blake as any sloo.
She was ful moore blisful on to see
Than is the newe pere-jonette tree,   140
And softer than the wolle is of a wether.
And by hir girdel heeng a purs of lether,
Tasseled with silk, and perled with latoun.
In al this world, to seken up and doun,
There nis no man so wys that koude thenche   145
So gay a popelote or swich a wenche.

- What impression of the young wife do we get from the comparisons to birds and animals and the natural world? Discuss not only what we are told about Alison's appearance, but why Chaucer might have chosen those particular details and comparisons. Why does he choose to compare her to certain creatures? Do we learn as much about her personality as we do about her appearance?
- Look again at the couplet on lines 161–2. How does this summary of her attractions pinpoint the wife's a) attractiveness, b) social status and c) power (or lack of it) in medieval society? (A yeoman is a working man – possibly wealthy, but definitely lower class.)
- Introductory descriptions of beautiful ladies were common in romantic tales (like the Knight's Tale, which precedes this one). But this beauty is no lady; how has Chaucer made you aware of this?

147–8	**Ful brighter ... yforged newe** her complexion glowed more brightly than any gold coin newly forged in the Tower [where the Mint was]	
149	**yerne** lively	
150	**swalwe ... berne** swallow [a shrill bird] perched on a barn [she's no cooing dove]	
151	**thereto** furthermore	
	make game prance about	
153	**bragot or the meeth** intoxicating drinks made with cider or ale and honey [She makes men's senses reel.]	
154	**hoord ... heeth** hoard of apples stored in hay or heather [good enough to bite]	
155	**winsinge ... colt** restless and lively as a young colt	

156	**long ... bolt** tall and upright as a mast and straight as an arrow [Working people quickly became bent and lame as they grew older.]
158	**brood ... bokeler** large as the centre boss of a small shield [The wealthy carpenter could indulge his wife's liking for showy ornament.]
160	**primerole, a piggesnie** a primrose [emphasising her fleeting young beauty], a little piglet [sweet and cuddlesome; modern idiom might be 'hugely fanciable']
161–2	**for any lord ... to wedde** for any lord to take to his bed, or for any good yeoman to marry [Note that the marriage is a second thought.]

Her glowing complexion, loud singing, frolicsome manner, and other aspects of her person are described.

Ful brighter was the shining of hir hewe
Than in the Tour the noble yforged newe.
But of hir song, it was as loude and yerne
As any swalwe sittinge on a berne.   150
Therto she koude skippe and make game,
As any kide or calf folwinge his dame.
Hir mouth was sweete as bragot or the meeth,
Or hoord of apples leyd in hey or heeth.
Winsinge she was, as is a joly colt,   155
Long as a mast, and upright as a bolt.
A brooch she baar upon hir lowe coler,
As brood as is the boos of a bokeler.
Hir shoes were laced on hir legges hye,
She was a primerole, a piggesnie,   160
For any lord to leggen in his bedde,
Or yet for any good yeman to wedde.

- Although the adjective 'hende' had commonly been used to describe fine young knights in courtly love romances, this would-be lover can hardly be called a 'gentil knight'. How does the behaviour described in lines 164–73 indicate this?
- Look carefully at all that the wife says and does in these lines. What sort of impression do you gain of her character and motivation? Chaucer deliberately omits any indication of exactly what Nicholas says to make her change her mind. Why might this be?
- How does the simile in line 174 seem in keeping with the earlier description of the wife?
- Working with a partner, discuss the respective merits of the carpenter and Nicholas as suitable partners for a young wife.

163	**Now ... the cas** Now, sir, this is how things turned out
165	**Fil ... pleye** began to flirt, mess about
166	**Oseneye** Osney [Then a small village near Oxford, now part of it; there was an abbey there, and clearly John is regularly employed to do work there.]
167	**clerkes ... queynte** students are so wily and crafty
168	**prively** furtively
	queynte her nice/dainty little bit [her private parts]
169	**Ywis ... I spille** You know, if I can't have my way, I'll perish, darling, with secret love for you
171	**heeld ... haunchebones** grabbed her hard round the hips
172	**al atones** right this minute
174–5	**she sproong ... faste awey** she leapt away like a young colt under restraint [trave: a frame used when shoeing lively horses] and quickly twisted her head away
177	**lat be** let be, stop it
178	**harrow** help
179	**do wey ... curteisie** shift your hands, if you please
180	**mercy** [The traditional plea of a suitor.]
181	**profred him so faste** offered attentions and love so earnestly
183	**Seint Thomas of Kent** [She seems to see nothing odd about swearing by the holy St Thomas Becket that she will betray her husband.]
184–5	**wol been ... wel espie** would be his to command when she found the right moment

One day the carpenter is away from home; Nicholas grabs Alison, telling her he's dying for love.
After an initial token protest, she is soon won over by Nicholas' sweet talking.

Now, sire, and eft, sire, so bifel the cas,
That on a day this hende Nicholas
Fil with this yonge wyf to rage and pleye,   165
Whil that hir housbonde was at Oseneye,
As clerkes ben ful subtil and ful queynte;
And prively he caughte hire by the queynte,
And seyde, 'Ywis, but if ich have my wille,
For deerne love of thee, lemman, I spille.'   170
And heeld hire harde by the haunchebones,
And seide, 'Lemman, love me al atones,
Or I wol dyen, also God me save!'
   And she sproong as a colt dooth in the trave,
And with hir heed she wryed faste awey,   175
And seide, 'I wol nat kisse thee, by my fey!
Why, lat be,' quod she, 'lat be, Nicholas,
Or I wol crie "out, harrow" and "allas"!
Do wey youre handes, for youre curteisie!'
   This Nicholas gan mercy for to crye,   180
And spak so faire, and profred him so faste,
That she hir love him graunted atte laste,
And swoor hir ooth, by Seint Thomas of Kent,
That she wol been at his comandement,
Whan that she may hir leiser wel espie.   185

- Make a list of all that Nicholas says and does during his courtship of Alison, from line 163 to 198. How does he treat Alison? And what is his attitude to John, her husband? How is his music used here to punctuate the scene? Would it be true to say that Nicholas is a self-satisfied young man?
- Religious observance and regular church-going were an accepted part of everyone's life in the fourteenth century. The spiritual value of this was clearly not always the most important factor. What proof of this do you find here and on previous pages? Make a chart, as the tale progresses, of the attitude to church and religion revealed by the various characters, and by the tale itself, at specific points in the story.

187–8   **but ye waite ... nam but deed** unless you're patient and careful I know I'm as good as dead

189   **ful deerne** really secretive [We have been told in line 92 that Nicholas is an expert at 'deerne love'.]

190–1   **a clerk ... bigile** a scholar has really wasted his time if he can't deceive a carpenter [The antagonism between university students and townspeople was a well-known facet of Oxford life; see page 91.]

196   **thakked ... lendes** patted her bottom

199   **fil it thus** so it happened

200   **Cristes owene werkes** to do Christ's work [attend the church service]

201   **haliday** holy day

202–3   **hir forheed ... leet hir werk** her face [forehead] shone as bright as day, since she washed it when she finished working [Her shining outward appearance belies her inner deceitfulness; Chaucer seems to use the word 'work' ironically.]

Alison warns him, however, of her husband's jealousy, and Nicholas promises he will find some
way of tricking the carpenter. She goes off to church, while he plays his psaltery.

'Myn housbonde is so ful of jalousie
That but ye waite wel and been privee,
I woot right wel I nam but deed,' quod she.
'Ye moste been ful deerne, as in this cas.'
    'Nay, therof care thee noght,' quod Nicholas.   190
'A clerk hadde litherly biset his while,
But if he koude a carpenter bigile.'
    And thus they been accorded and ysworn
To waite a time as I have told biforn.
Whan Nicholas had doon thus everideel,   195
And thakked hire aboute the lendes weel,
He kiste hire sweete and taketh his sautrie,
And pleyeth faste, and maketh melodie.
    Thanne fil it thus, that to the parissh chirche,
Cristes owene werkes for to wirche,   200
This goode wyf went on an haliday.
Hir forheed shoon as bright as any day,
So was it wasshen whan she leet hir werk.

- 'Clerk' is a term used quite loosely in the fourteenth century, meaning one who can read and write – sometimes a priest (though not all rural parish priests were literate at that time), a scholar or a student. Not all clerks became churchmen: some were administrators, or lawyers. Many had little interest in religion; the Clerk of the General Prologue is more interested in philosophy than church writings. How interested in religion does Absolon, the parish clerk, seem to be?
- Compare and contrast the presentation of the two clerks, Nicholas and Absolon. Highlight the similarities and differences between them. Which seems to you the more attractive? Which one is most clearly depicted? (Absalom [or Absolon], David's son in the Bible, was traditionally the most beautiful of men.)
- Without saying anything unpleasant about him, Chaucer somehow conveys the idea that Absolon is a slightly absurd figure. How does he achieve this? It may help to read some of the lines aloud.

204	**parissh clerk** a layman who assisted the priest in church ceremonies, or with clerical duties	
206	**crul** curly	
207	**strouted ... brode** stuck out like a fan round his face	
208	**joly shode** splendid parting [Absolon's hair is clearly his pride and joy.]	
209	**rode** complexion	
	greye as goos grey as a goose [rather a silly, pop-eyed bird]	
210	**with Poules ... his shoos** with an elaborately cut design like a church window on his shoes	
211	**hoses rede ... fetisly** he tripped along most elegantly in his red stockings	
212	**smal and proprely** tightly and tastefully	
213	**kirtel ... waget** a tunic of light blue	
214	**ful faire ... pointes set** stoutly and plentifully supplied with laces [as fastenings]	
215	**gay surplis** bright surplice	
216	**ris** bough or twig	

217	**mirie child** pleasant young fellow
218	**laten blood ... shave** he could let blood [a medical practice], clip hair and shave men [a useful part-time barber]
219	**maken a chartre ... acquitaunce** he drew up land deeds and legal settlements
220–2	**in twenty ... to and fro** he could dance at least twenty different ways – but only after the Oxford style, waving his legs backwards and forwards
223	**smal rubible** little fiddle
224	**loud quinible** penetrating high voice
225	**giterne** form of guitar
226–8	**in al the toun ... tappestere was** throughout the town there wasn't a single inn or tavern, with a lively barmaid, that he hadn't graced with his presence [The triple negative, 'nas', 'ne', 'ne', stresses his determined socialising.]
229	**somdeel squaymous** quite squeamish
230	**of speche daungerous** fastidious in his speech

Absolon, a parish clerk, is introduced; carefully, even fussily, dressed, a keen dancer, musical, sociable and rather squeamish.

Now was ther of that chirche a parissh clerk,
The which that was ycleped Absolon.   205
Crul was his heer, and as the gold it shoon,
And strouted as a fanne large and brode;
Ful streight and evene lay his joly shode.
His rode was reed, his eyen greye as goos.
With Poules window corven on his shoos,   210
In hoses rede he wente fetisly.
Yclad he was ful smal and proprely
Al in a kirtel of a light waget;
Ful faire and thikke been the pointes set.
And therupon he hadde a gay surplis   215
As whit as is the blosme upon the ris.
A mirie child he was, so God me save.
Wel koude he laten blood and clippe and shave,
And maken a chartre of lond or acquitaunce.
In twenty manere koude he trippe and daunce   220
After the scole of Oxenforde tho,
And with his legges casten to and fro,
And pleyen songes on a smal rubible;
Therto he song som time a loud quinible;
And as wel koude he pleye on a giterne.   225
In al the toun nas brewhous ne taverne
That he ne visited with his solas,
Ther any gailard tappestere was.
But sooth to seyn, he was somdeel squaymous
Of farting, and of speche daungerous.   230

• Chaucer has already set Absolon up as a figure of fun, with an elevated idea of his own attractiveness and status. His pompous conceit begs to be deflated. Write two paragraphs, one showing how Absolon sees himself, the other showing how the reader interprets the information differently.

• Great attention has been given to the clothing and outward appearance of at least two of the characters introduced. How effectively have such descriptions revealed character? Are there times when superficial appearances of Alison, Nicholas or Absolon conceal what lies beneath? Select particular details to justify your answer.

• Discuss whether Absolon's behaviour seems appropriate in a parish clerk and servant of the church.

231	**jolif ... and gay** jolly and bright
232–3	**Gooth with ... faste** Goes up and down the church swinging the censer and liberally dousing the women with perfume [The repetition of 'sencer' and 'sensinge' emphasises the over-zealous nature of Absolon's manner, and his enthusiastic regard for pretty women.]
236	**a mirie lyf** a wonderful way to pass time
237	**likerous** sexy [suggests a different side to her]
238–9	**if she ... hente anon** if she were a mouse and he a cat, he'd have caught her right away
241–2	**swich ... noon offringe** such an agony of love, he took no donations from any of them

243	**curteisie** good manners [The money is for the church, not him – an absurd gesture.]
246	**for paramours ... to wake** for love's sake he decided to stay awake all night
249	**after cokkes hadde ycrowe** after cockcrow [dawn]
250	**dressed ... shot-windowe** set himself up by a hinged window [Note this window opens.]
251	**carpenteris wal** wall of the carpenter's house [It's important to the success of this tale that Chaucer's audience is able to visualise clearly what happens where.]

During his church duties Absolon looks amorously at all the young women, particularly the carpenter's wife. So besotted is he, he refuses to take offerings from any of them. That night, in a fervour of love, he takes his guitar and takes up position outside Alison's window to serenade her.

This Absolon, that jolif was and gay,
Gooth with a sencer on the haliday,
Sensinge the wives of the parisshe faste;
And many a lovely look on hem he caste,
And namely on this carpenteris wyf.   235
To looke on hire him thoughte a mirie lyf,
She was so propre and sweete and likerous.
I dar wel seyn if she hadde been a mous,
And he a cat, he wolde hire hente anon.
This parissh clerk, this joly Absolon,   240
Hath in his herte swich a love-longinge
That of no wyf took he noon offringe;
For curteisie, he seide, he wolde noon.
  The moone, whan it was night, ful brighte shoon,
And Absolon his giterne hath ytake,   245
For paramours he thoghte for to wake.
And forth he gooth, jolif and amorous,
Til he cam to the carpenters hous
A litel after cokkes hadde ycrowe,
And dressed him up by a shot-windowe   250
That was upon the carpenteris wal.

- The little scene described between lines 244 and 261 offers a good opportunity for dramatic presentation. How successfully does Chaucer suggest Absolon's absurdity? How do you think John, the carpenter, reacts? And exactly what tone of voice do you imagine Alison uses when she speaks those few words on line 261? Working in a group experiment with different ways of delivering the lines.
- In lines 256–62 we learn the names of the 'main' characters for the first time. Discuss why it might be that Chaucer chooses to reveal their names here, when they are in their marital bed, and the words 'wife' and 'husband' are in close juxtaposition to 'Alison' and 'John'.
- Absolon sees himself as a 'courtly lover' (see pages 6–7 for information). How does Chaucer make him seem totally mistaken here? As you read on note where else the tale offers comparisons with more romantic stories.

252	**gentil and smal** genteel and high [rather refined – in keeping with his image of himself], a bit effeminate
253–4	**Now deere lady … wole rewe on me** Now dear lady, if it pleases you I beg you to take pity on me [The romantic ideal of a lover pining for love of his lady, begging for a favour, is the part Absolon plays here.]
255	**ful wel … giterninge** nicely harmonising with his strumming
258–9	**What … boures wal** Hey, Alison, can't you hear Absolon singing under our bedroom window?
260	**therwithal** thereupon, forthwith
261	**Yis … every deel** Yes, God knows, John, I can hear every note
262	**This … than weel** and so it goes on – what more would you have?

264	**woweth** woos
	wo bigon woebegone, utterly miserable
266	**kembeth … him gay** combs his luxuriant hair and dresses in his best clothes
267	**meenes and brocage** go-betweens to speak on his behalf [a technique used by bashful courtly lovers]
268	**hir owene page** her own faithful servant
269	**brokkinge** quavering, trilling
270	**piment, meeth, and spiced ale** sweetened, spiced wines and ale
271	**wafres … the gleede** crispy biscuits [gaufrettes], piping hot, fresh from the oven
272	**for she was … meede** since she was a townswoman [*i.e.* practical] he offered money

Absolon begins his serenade. The carpenter is woken by the noise, and so is his wife. Absolon continues to woo her in every way he can think of – with gifts, songs, even money.

He singeth in his vois gentil and smal,
'Now, deere lady, if thy wille be,
I praye yow that ye wole rewe on me,'
Ful wel acordaunt to his giterninge.   255
  This carpenter awook, and herde him singe,
And spak unto his wyf, and seide anon,
'What! Alison! herestow nat Absolon,
That chaunteth thus under oure boures wal?'
And she answerde hir housbonde therwithal,   260
'Yis, God woot, John, I heere it every deel.'
  This passeth forth; what wol ye bet than weel?
Fro day to day this joly Absolon
So woweth hire that him is wo bigon.
He waketh al the night and al the day;   265
He kembeth his lokkes brode, and made him gay;
He woweth hire by meenes and brocage,
And swoor he wolde been hir owene page;
He singeth, brokkinge as a nightingale;
He sente hire piment, meeth, and spiced ale,   270
And wafres, piping hoot out of the gleede;
And, for she was of town, he profred meede.

- Absolon has imitated the behaviour of a courtly lover in his attempts to woo Alison; Nicholas is far more direct (and successful) in his approach to what he's after. Does Chaucer make him seem more or less despicable as a result? Is there any proof, in the tale so far, that the elaborate trickery is as enjoyable to Nicholas as the final conquest of Alison?
- These lines act as a signal to the audience that the cast has been assembled, their relationships explained and the action is about to begin. Discuss what you think is likely to happen next. As the tale develops, consider how correct you were in your surmise. You may find Nicholas' imaginative plan and tricks played by other characters produce unexpected results.
- This tale is supposedly being told by a drunken Miller. Note any language, used so far, which suggests this is really the case. Add to your list as the tale progresses.

273–4   **som folk ... gentillesse** some are won by wealth, some by tough treatment, some by courtesy [The subject of how to woo a woman is raised several times in *The Canterbury Tales* – most particularly in the Wife of Bath's Tale.]

275   **lightnesse and maistrie** dexterity and skill

276   **pleyeth Herodes ... hye** acted the part of Herod on a high platform [In mystery plays a part usually taken by a dominant, strong-voiced, masterful actor.]

277   **what availleth ... this cas** what good did all this do him

279   **blowe the bukkes horn** whistle at the moon [*literally*: try to blow a buck's horn – a futile gesture]

280   **ne hadde ... scorn** he achieved nothing but contempt for all his efforts

281   **ape** fool

282   **al his ... jape** makes a joke of all his earnest wooing

283   **Ful sooth** very true

284–5   **Alwey ... to be looth** A cunning lover nearby can always makes a distant one loathed

286–8   **For though ... in his light** For even though Absolon might feel mad or furious because he was unable to see her, Nicholas was so close at hand that he prevented her even noticing him

289   **ber thee wel** show us how clever you are [a hint to the audience that the action is about to begin]

Absolon even acts the role of Herod on stage, to impress her. All to no avail: she loves Nicholas. Alison feels nothing but contempt for Absolon – she makes a joke of the parish clerk's attentions. Chaucer comments on the value of propinquity when it comes to love affairs.

For som folk wol ben wonnen for richesse,
And somme for strokes, and somme for gentillesse.
Somtime, to shewe his lightnesse and maistrie,   275
He pleyeth Herodes upon a scaffold hye.
But what availleth him as in this cas?
She loveth so this hende Nicholas
That Absolon may blowe the bukkes horn;
He ne hadde for his labour but a scorn.   280
And thus she maketh Absolon hire ape,
And al his ernest turneth til a jape.
Ful sooth is this proverbe, it is no lie,
Men seyn right thus, 'Alwey the nie slie
Maketh the ferre leeve to be looth.'   285
For though that Absolon be wood or wrooth,
By cause that he fer was from hire sight,
This nie Nicholas stood in his light.
Now ber thee wel, thou hende Nicholas,
For Absolon may waille and singe 'allas.'   290

- As the plan unfolds, bear in mind that it must somehow allow Nicholas and Alison to enjoy a sexual relationship without jeopardising her position as wife and his as favoured lodger. Although it might seem that Nicholas and Alison could simply get together during John's absence, remember there was little privacy in medieval households – and there are two servants. Part of Nicholas' enjoyment will be related to tricking John the carpenter.
- Should we feel sorry for the 'sely' carpenter? ('Sely' could be used as a term of approval, meaning holy, unworldly.) Look again at the comment Chaucer makes in lines 119–24.
- What do these plans reveal about Alison's character?

291	**bifel it** it happened	303	**a day or tweye** a day or two [he doesn't intend to go hungry]
292	**Osenay** [presumably to do work at the abbey]	304	**bad hire** told her
294	**Acorded been to this conclusioun** had come to this agreement	305	**axed** asked
		306–7	**she niste … nat with ye** she didn't know [*abbrev.* 'ne wiste'] where he was – she hadn't laid eyes on him all day
295	**shapen him a wile** devise a clever trick		
296	**sely** foolish, innocent, gullible	308–10	**She trowed … that mighte falle** She believed he must be sick, for he made no reply to her maid when she called him, whatever the message might be
300	**withouten wordes mo** without another word spoken		
301	**tarie** hesitate		
302	**ful softe** most quietly, secretly		

John has to be away one Saturday, and Nicholas concocts an elaborate trick which will allow Alison to spend the night with him. Firstly he stays in his room, well supplied with food and drink. Alison is to say, if asked, that she thinks he must be sick.

And so bifel it on a Saterday,
This carpenter was goon til Osenay;
And hende Nicholas and Alisoun
Acorded been to this conclusioun,
That Nicholas shal shapen him a wile   295
This sely jalous housbonde to bigile;
And if so be the game wente aright,
She sholde slepen in his arm al night,
For this was his desir and hire also.
And right anon, withouten wordes mo,   300
This Nicholas no lenger wolde tarie,
But dooth ful softe unto his chambre carie
Bothe mete and drinke for a day or tweye,
And to hire housbonde bad hire for to seye,
If that he axed after Nicholas,   305
She sholde seye she niste where he was,
Of al that day she saugh him nat with ye;
She trowed that he was in maladie,
For for no cry hir maide koude him calle,
He nolde answere for thing that mighte falle.   310

Sudden and inexplicable death had become frighteningly common during the plague years, which reached England in 1348; further outbreaks occurred until the late 1360s. The precariousness of life is indicated in lines 321–2, and any signs of unusual illness might well worry a fearful man like John.

- Chaucer has already mentioned Nicholas' skill at 'foretelling' (lines 84–90). As the student's plan develops, the importance of this information becomes clear. By what means, in lines 315–39, is the audience made aware of the attitude of the wealthy peasant towards his lodger?
- The servant plays a very small part in events, and yet he is by no means a colourless character. What do you learn about him from lines 326–35?

311	**thilke** this	320	**ful tikel** full of uncertainty
312	**stille** silently	321–2	**I saugh ... wirche** today I saw a man carried to church as a corpse, who had been fit and working last Monday
	what him leste what he pleased		
315	**This sely ... greet merveile** the naive carpenter was most puzzled [Nicholas, a scholar, is already regarded as a 'different 'sort of person by the labourer.]		
		325	**Looke ... boldely** see how things are and tell me straight
		328	**as that he were wood** like a mad thing, frenziedly
316	**him eyle** be wrong with him	332	**hole he foond ... bord** found a hole set low on the door
317	**adrad** afraid		
318	**stondeth nat aright** things aren't right	333	**wont ... crepe** had a habit of slipping in
319	**shilde** forbid	334	**ful depe** very intently
	deide sodeinly suddenly dropped dead		

All Saturday Nicholas stays silently in his room. Finally the carpenter, superstitious and fearful, sends his servant to find out what's wrong. Receiving no answer to his shouts, the servant peeps through a hole in the door, and catches sight of Nicholas.

This passeth forth al thilke Saterday,
That Nicholas stille in his chambre lay,
And eet and sleep, or dide what him leste,
Til Sonday, that the sonne gooth to reste.
This sely carpenter hath greet merveile   315
Of Nicholas, or what thing mighte him eyle,
And seide, 'I am adrad, by Seint Thomas,
It stondeth nat aright with Nicholas.
God shilde that he deide sodeinly!
This world is now ful tikel, sikerly.   320
I saugh to-day a cors yborn to chirche
That now, on Monday last, I saugh him wirche.
Go up,' quod he unto his knave anoon,
'Clepe at his dore, or knokke with a stoon.
Looke how it is, and tel me boldely.'   325
   This knave gooth him up ful sturdily,
And at the chambre dore whil that he stood,
He cride and knokked as that he were wood,
'What! how! what do ye, maister Nicholay?
How may ye slepen al the longe day?'   330
But al for noght, he herde nat a word.
An hole he foond, ful lowe upon a bord,
Ther as the cat was wont in for to crepe,
And at that hole he looked in ful depe,
And at the laste he hadde of him a sight.   335

- The carpenter reveals his train of thought very clearly in lines 341–56. Working in a group, prepare a dramatic presentation of the whole of this section, showing particularly how Chaucer's words reveal the carpenter's attitude and feelings.
- How does John's attitude to religion seem to differ from that revealed earlier by Alison, Absolon and Nicholas? Remember the chart you began on page 30 and update it.

336 **evere caping upright** fixedly gaping upwards, open-mouthed

337 **as he had kiked** as if looking at

339 **what array** what state
ilke this

340 **blessen him bigan** began to bless himself

341 **Seinte Frideswide** an eighth century abbess and the patron saint of Oxford

342 **woot litel what him shal bitide** little knows what will happen to him [Both John and Nicholas are in for some surprises before the tale ends; but that is not quite what the carpenter means here.]

343 **astromie** astronomy [This may be as close as John can get to the pronunciation.]

344 **woodnesse or ... agonie** madness or mental anguish

345–8 **I thoghte ... bileve kan** I always thought something like this would happen. Men should not try to uncover God's hidden mysteries. The uneducated man is the blessed one, because he only knows what he's been told to believe [*i.e.* what he has been taught by his parish priest in the words of the Creed – he doesn't choose to investigate anything too closely; John's ready belief will soon prove to be his downfall]

349 **so ferde** the same thing happened

350 **for to prye ... bifalle** to star-gaze in order to discover what would happen in the future

351 **marle-pit** clay pit [a well-known story illustrating the foolishness of scholarly men]

354 **reweth soore** feel very sorry for

355 **shal be rated of** shall be scolded for

356 **if that I may** if it is given to me to do this [John clearly feels he has the moral upper hand.]

Nicholas is staring fixedly heavenwards. The carpenter fears that too much studying of astrology has brought some dreadful seizure upon Nicholas. He believes it is unwise to know too much and decides he must save him.

This Nicholas sat evere caping upright,
As he had kiked on the newe moone.
Adoun he gooth, and tolde his maister soone
In what array he saugh this ilke man.
  This carpenter to blessen him bigan,   340
And seide, 'Help us, Seinte Frideswide!
A man woot lite what him shal bitide.
This man is falle, with his astromie,
In some woodnesse or in some agonie.
I thoghte ay wel how that it sholde be!   345
Men sholde nat knowe of Goddes privetee.
Ye, blessed be alwey a lewed man
That noght but oonly his bileve kan!
So ferde another clerk with astromie;
He walked in the feeldes, for to prye   350
Upon the sterres, what ther sholde bifalle,
Til he was in a marle-pit yfalle;
He saugh nat that. But yet, by Seint Thomas,
Me reweth soore of hende Nicholas.
He shal be rated of his studiyng,   355
If that I may by Jhesus, hevene king!

- From his reactions to Nicholas' apparent seizure what do you learn about the carpenter's character and his attitude to the spiritual and cerebral parts of life?
- Look closely at the way in which Christian religion is mixed with more general fear of the supernatural on this page. Look back on this later and see how Chaucer uses this to prepare the way for what is to follow.

357 **underspore** lever upwards

358 **hevest up the dore** heave the door off its hinges

359 **as I gesse** if I know anything about it

361 **strong ... nones** strong lad – just the man for the job [uncannily like the Miller of the General Prologue]

362–3 **And by ... fil anon** And he grabbed the door by the hinges directly; it fell to the floor at once. [Clearly the carpenter and his servant are used to fixing problems promptly by physical solutions; notice how the sound of line 362 imitates physical effort.]

364 **ay** unceasingly

365 **caped upward** gaped aloft

366 **wende ... despeir** believed him to be in despair [Despair was one of the deadly sins.]

367–8 **hente him ... cride spitously** grabbed him vehemently by the shoulders, shook him hard and cried out fiercely [Notice how the strength of words and rhythm here captures the mood of the scene.]

370 **thenk on Cristes passioun** remember Christ sacrificed himself to save mankind from hell [Such belief would give Nicholas hope, and save him from the damnation of his soul brought on by despair.]

371 **I crouche ... wightes** I make the sign of the cross to protect you from evil spirits and ghosts

372 **the night-spel** a magic charm to ward off evil spirits [His words on lines 377–8 are a mixture of Christian prayer and superstition.]

372 **anon-rightes** straightaway

375 **Benedight** St Benedict [founder of the Benedictine order of monks]

376 **wikked wight** wicked person

377 **for nightes verye** from night dangers

the white *pater-noster* the Lord's Prayer [or pater noster] was recited as a sure protection [or 'white' magic] against all evil

378 **Where ... soster?** Where were you when we needed you, St Peter's sister? [An imaginary good spirit – John's outburst is a splendid mixture of prayer and superstitious folly.]

With the help of his servant, Robin, John levers the door off its hinges and Robin smashes it down.
The carpenter does all he can, with prayers and making the sign of the cross, to rouse Nicholas
from his apparent trance.

Get me a staf, that I may underspore,
Whil that thou, Robin, hevest up the dore.
He shal out of his studiyng, as I gesse'—
And to the chambre dore he gan him dresse.   360
His knave was a strong carl for the nones,
And by the haspe he haaf it of atones;
Into the floor the dore fil anon.
    This Nicholas sat ay as stille as stoon,
And evere caped upward into the eir.   365
This carpenter wende he were in despeir,
And hente him by the sholdres mightily,
And shook him harde, and cride spitously,
'What! Nicholay! what, how! what, looke adoun!
Awak, and thenk on Cristes passioun!   370
I crouche thee from elves and fro wightes.'
Therwith the night-spel seide he anon-rightes
On foure halves of the hous aboute,
And on the thresshfold of the dore withoute:
'Jhesu Crist and Seint Benedight,   375
Blesse this hous from every wikked wight,
For nightes verye, the white *pater-noster*!
Where wentestow, Seinte Petres soster?'

- There is quite astounding audacity about Nicholas' plot. How does the clerk impress upon the gullible carpenter the solemnity and importance of what he has to tell?
- Analyse Nicholas' speech (lines 393–9) and decide why it would be likely to impress John so greatly. How does Chaucer indicate that John has swallowed the whole story?

380 Gan ... soore began to sigh bitterly

381 eftsoones yet again

382 What seistow? What are you talking about?

383 as we doon ... swinke as we do, we working men [*i.e.* not you bookish clerks]

385 in privetee in secret

387 noon oother no other

391 dore fast shette securely fastened his door [presumably mended and re-hung]

393 myn hooste lief and deere dearly beloved host [landlord]

394 thy trouthe your promise [A 'trouthe' was a most serious and binding oath.]

395 to no wight ... wreye you will betray this confidence to no other person

396 Cristes conseil confidential information from Christ himself [Nicholas has no moral scruples, neither about committing such blasphemy, nor about doing it in order to commit adultery with John's wife.]

397 forlore doomed

398 vengeaunce punishment

399 if thou ... wood if you betray me you will be made insane

401 Quod tho this sely man Then said this simple man ['sely' can mean foolish, but also 'innocent' and sometimes even 'holy']

401–4 nam no ... to child ne wyf I am no blabbermouth; nor, though I say it myself, do I care to pass on gossip. Say what you like, I shall never tell it to anyone, be they child nor wife [The number of negatives – 'nam no', 'nam nat' – are an indication of the fervour with which John promises to keep silent – and a suggestion that he is thoroughly taken in by the plausible young clerk.]

404 by him that harwed helle I swear it on the name of Christ who harrowed hell [Many medieval mystery plays dealt with the story of Christ's descent into hell after the crucifixion, to save the souls of the faithful, as decreed by the prophets.]

Finally Nicholas sighs bitterly, mutters ominously, and, after asking for a drink, tells John he has an important secret to reveal to him. He threatens John that if he reveals what is about to be told, the consequences will be dreadful. John promises he is no blabber mouth; he will not tell a soul.

And atte laste this hende Nicholas
Gan for to sik soore, and seide, 'Allas!   380
Shal al the world be lost eftsoones now?'
    This carpenter answerde, 'What seistow?
What! think on God, as we doon, men that swinke.'
    This Nicholas answerde, 'Fecche me drinke,
And after wol I speke in privetee   385
Of certein thing that toucheth me and thee.
I wol telle it noon oother man, certein.'
    This carpenter goth doun, and comth agein,
And broghte of mighty ale a large quart;
And whan that ech of hem had dronke his part,   390
This Nicholas his dore faste shette,
And doun the carpenter by him he sette.
    He seide, 'John myn hooste, lief and deere,
Thou shalt upon thy trouthe swere me heere
That to no wight thou shalt this conseil wreye;   395
For it is Cristes conseil that I seye,
And if thou telle it man, thou art forlore;
For this vengeaunce thou shalt han therfore,
That if thou wreye me, thou shalt be wood.'
    'Nay, Crist forbede it, for his hooly blood!'   400
Quod tho this sely man, 'I nam no labbe;
Ne, though I seye, I nam nat lief to gabbe.
Sey what thou wolt, I shal it nevere telle
To child ne wyf, by him that harwed helle!'

The building of Noah's ark was a popular subject for mystery plays, sometimes acted by the Shipwrights' Guild, sometimes the Carpenters'. It would appeal to the carpenter (who should, however, have known that there was only to be **one** flood).

- What do you make of John's reactions to Nicholas' story? Look back at the way he behaved in lines 366–78. How successfully does Nicholas make it both dramatic and plausible?
- Before reading on to the development of Nicholas' plan, discuss what he tells John here. How can this amazingly implausible yarn enable Nicholas to spend the night with Alison?
- Certainly the clerk seems knowledgeable about biblical matters. Does it seem wrong that he uses his knowledge, and John's ignorance, for immoral purposes? (Remember this is a fabliau – see page 7 for details – does that make a difference?)

---

406   **I have yfounde in myn astrologie** I have discovered through my astrological studies

408   **a Monday … night** on Monday, a quarter way through the night [The action so far has taken place on Sunday evening – see line 314.]

409   **wilde and wood** wild and frenzied

410   **half so greet … flood** Noah's flood was never half so vast [Medieval astronomy believed the position of the moon to be most important in regulating the extent of rainfall – and if the moon was in a position controlled by a 'water' sign of the zodiac, then heavy downpour was even more likely.]

412   **dreynt** engulfed by water
     hidous is the shour fearful is the downfall

413   **Thus shal … hir lyf** so shall all mankind drown and die [Nicholas is most grandiose in his story telling.]

416   **For sorwe of this he fil almoost adoun** So great was his sorrow at this that he almost collapsed

417   **Is ther no remedie in this cas?** Is there no way to prevent this?

418   **yis, for God** yes, by God

419–20   **If thou wolt … owene heed** If you follow the rules and advice you're given [by Nicholas himself, of course]. Don't try to take matters into your own hands.

421   **Salomon, that was ful trewe** [Solomon's name was often taken as a byword for wisdom.]

422   **Werk al … nat rewe** Take advice on all things and you won't live to regret it.

424–5   **I undertake … and me** I promise, even without masts or sails, that I shall save you, and her, and me [Even the credulous carpenter might realise that he can't build an ark or ship by the next night; Nicholas must come up with a scheme that seems just about plausible.]

426   **hastow nat** have you not
     Noe Noah

427   **biforn** in advance

428   **lorn** lost

429   **ful yoore ago** a long time ago

Nicholas says he has forewarning of a huge flood which will destroy mankind. John's first thought is for his wife. The clerk promises that if John follows his instructions to the letter he can save himself, Alison and Nicholas too, just as Noah saved his family.

'Now John,' quod Nicholas, 'I wol nat lie;   405
I have yfounde in myn astrologie,
As I have looked in the moone bright,
That now a Monday next, at quarter night,
Shal falle a reyn, and that so wilde and wood,
That half so greet was nevere Noes flood.   410
This world' he seide, 'in lasse than an hour
Shal al be dreynt, so hidous is the shour.
Thus shal mankinde drenche, and lese hir lyf.'
   This carpenter answerde, 'Allas, my wyf!
And shal she drenche? allas, myn Alisoun!'   415
For sorwe of this he fil almoost adoun,
And seide, 'Is ther no remedie in this cas?'
   'Why, yis, for Gode,' quod hende Nicholas,
'If thou wolt werken after loore and reed.
Thou mayst nat werken after thyn owene heed;   420
For thus seith Salomon, that was ful trewe,
"Werk al by conseil, and thou shalt nat rewe."
And if thou werken wolt by good conseil,
I undertake, withouten mast and seil,
Yet shal I saven hire and thee and me.   425
Hastow nat herd hou saved was Noe,
Whan that oure Lord hadde warned him biforn
That al the world with water sholde be lorn?'
   'Yis,' quod this carpenter, 'ful yoore ago.'

'Hastow nat herd hou saved was Noe ...?'

51

- This carefully planned plot still leaves a number of questions unanswered for the audience. How do you think these preparations for a non-existent flood are going to help Nicholas?
- What indications are there in lines 430–54 that Nicholas has anticipated possible obstacles to the success of his plan, and devised ways to overcome them?
- Does Nicholas seem to be more skilful as a storyteller and inventive fantasist than as a courtly lover? Why might this be?

431 **sorwe of Noe with his felaweshipe** the difficulty Noah and his crew encountered

432 **Er that he ... to shipe** Before he could get his wife on board [The York Mystery play of 'The Flood' shows Mrs Noah grimly refusing to get on board the ark without her cronies and her best saucepans, as the floods rise.]

433 **Him hadde be levere** he would have preferred

dar wel undertake I'm quite sure

434 **thilke** this

434–5 **than alle ... allone** he'd have preferred her to have her own boat, even more than keeping all his black wethers [sheep]

436 **woostou** do you know

437 **asketh haste** requires speed

437–8 **of an hastif ... maken tariyng** something that requires speedy action doesn't allow for too much talking or hanging about [Even John might have begun questioning Nicholas' tale if he'd had time to think about it.]

439 **Anon ... this in** straightaway go and fetch here to this lodging house

440 **kneding trogh** [long wooden trough for bread or wine-making]

or ellis a kymelin or else a brewing tub

442 **we mowe swimme as in a barge** we can float as if in a barge

443 **han therinne** put in them

vitaille suffisant sufficient supplies

444 **fy on the remenant!** never mind what comes later!

445 **aslake** seep away

446 **aboute prime** around early morning, nine o'clock

447 **may nat wite** must not learn

448 **ne eek** nor also [and neither]

449 **axe nat** don't ask

451–2 **Suffiseth thee ... Noe hadde** It's enough for you to know, unless you're out of your mind, that you have been given as great a blessing from God as was given to Noah

453 **out of doute** be sure

454 **speed thee heer-aboute** hurry back here soon

He also reminds John of the trouble Noah had with his wife. The plan unfolds: speed is of the essence. John must find three troughs or barrels, each large enough for one person, and load them with a day's supply of food and drink. By early next day the flood will be over. Only John and his wife may be saved – John is not to question why this has been decreed.

'Hastou nat herd,' quod Nicholas, 'also   430
The sorwe of Noe with his felaweshipe,
Er that he mighte gete his wyf to shipe?
Him hadde be levere, I dar wel undertake
At thilke time, than alle his wetheres blake
That she hadde had a ship hirself allone.   435
And therfore, woostou what is best to doone?
This asketh haste, and of an hastif thing
Men may nat preche or maken tariyng.
Anon go gete us faste into this in
A kneding trogh, or ellis a kymelin,   440
For ech of us, but looke that they be large,
In which we mowe swimme as in a barge,
And han therinne vitaille suffisant
But for a day: fy on the remenant!
The water shal aslake and goon away   445
Aboute prime upon the nexte day.
But Robin may nat wite of this, thy knave,
Ne eek thy maide Gille I may nat save;
Axe nat why, for though thou aske me,
I wol nat tellen Goddes privetee.   450
Suffiseth thee, but if thy wittes madde,
To han as greet a grace as Noe hadde.
Thy wyf shal I wel saven, out of doute.
Go now thy wey, and speed thee heer-aboute.

'A kneding trogh, or ellis a kymelin'

- Every instruction, every description of how to prepare for the flood and what will happen after it, is based on total fantasy. Why has Chaucer included it at this point in the tale? In what way does it add anything to your enjoyment of the narrative? Or your understanding of the characters involved? Discuss these points before you move on.
- What aspect of John's character is being appealed to in lines 473–4?

456	**ygeten** obtained		466	**grete shour** great downfall
457	**shaltow** you must		467–8	**Thanne shaltou ... hire drake**
	in the roof in the rafters			Then I promise, you shall sail
458	**of oure purveiaunce spye** can see			along as merrily as a white duck
	what we're planning			swims after her drake [John is
460	**oure vitaille faire in hem yleid**			likened to the following duck, not
	carefully stowed our supplies in			the more powerful drake.]
	them		469	**clepe** call out
461–2	**smite the corde ... that we may**			**how** hallo there [in this context]
	go cut the rope in half when the		470	**be mirie** be happy
	waters come, so that we are free to			**wol passe anon** will be over soon
	escape		472	**I se thee wel for it is day** I can see
463	**an heigh, upon the gable** high			you clearly for day is dawning
	up at the gable end		473–4	**lordes al oure lyf ... Noe and his**
464	**gardin-ward** the garden side of			**wyf** the world will belong to us as
	the house			it did to Noah and his wife
465	**frely passen forth oure way**			
	easily sail away			

The tubs must also contain axes, to cut the binding ropes. When the floods come, they will break through the roof, ready to sail away across the garden, chatting cheerily as they bob along. Afterwards they will be lords of all the world.

But whan thou hast, for hire and thee and me,   455
Ygeten us thise kneding tubbes thre,
Thanne shaltow hange hem in the roof ful hye,
That no man of oure purveiaunce spye.
And whan thou thus hast doon, as I have seid,
And hast oure vitaille faire in hem yleid,   460
And eek an ax, to smite the corde atwo,
Whan that the water comth, that we may go,
And breke an hole an heigh, upon the gable,
Unto the gardin-ward, over the stable,
That we may frely passen forth oure way,   465
Whan that the grete shour is goon away,
Thanne shaltou swimme as mirie, I undertake,
As dooth the white doke after hire drake.
Thanne wol I clepe, "How, Alison! how, John!
Be mirie, for the flood wol passe anon."   470
And thou wolt seyn, "Hail, maister Nicholay!
Good morwe, I se thee wel, for it is day."
And thanne shul we be lordes al oure lyf
Of al the world, as Noe and his wyf.

- Does this callous and efficient method of tricking the carpenter detract from the humour and ingenuity of the tale?
- Does John's obvious concern for his wife make him an object for sympathy? And how do you view the fact that he tells Alison everything, in spite of what he said in lines 401–4?
- What does Chaucer reveal about Alison's character from the few words she speaks here?

Line	Gloss
475	**o thing** one thing
476	**wel avised** be sure to take warning
477	**ben entred** go aboard [the tubs]
478–9	**noon of us ... his preyere** none of us must speak a single word, nor call out, nor cry – except in prayer [The use of double negatives stresses the vehemence of the clerk's command here – and the reason for this requirement, and that on lines 481–2, will soon become obvious.]
480	**Goddes owene heeste deere** God's own most important command
481	**hange fer atwinne** hang [in your tubs] far apart
482	**for that** so that
482–3	**bitwixe yow ... shal in deede** no sin [sexual contact] between the pair of you – neither visual nor physical contact
485	**ben alle aslepe** are all asleep
487	**abiding Goddes grace** awaiting God's mercy
488–9	**no lenger ... sermoning** no time to spend on further sermonising
490	**'Sende the wise, and sey no thing'** 'A word is enough to the wise man' – a proverbial saying [He flatters John by calling him 'wise' and also prevents him from asking too many awkward questions.]
491	**it needeth thee nat teche** there's no need to teach you further
492	**I the biseche** I beg you
493	**sely carpenter** foolish, gullible, carpenter
494	**weylawey** woe is me
495	**his privetee** his secret
496	**she was war** she was already aware, forewarned
497	**what al this queynte cast was for to seye** what this crafty plot was all about
498	**nathelees she ferde as she wolde deye** she acted as if she was in mortal danger
499	**go forth thy wey anon** off you go immediately
500	**we ben dede echon** each one of us will die

Not a word must be spoken, and Alison and her husband must keep their tubs far apart during the night of the flood. When everyone is asleep the three of them will creep into their tubs and await God's mercy. The distraught carpenter is sent off with his assignments; he tells his wife Nicholas' tale. She pretends to be afraid and begs her husband to go and do what he must to save their lives.

But of o thing I warne thee ful right: 475
Be wel avised on that ilke night
That we ben entred into shippes bord,
That noon of us ne speke nat a word,
Ne clepe, ne crie, but be in his preyere;
For it is Goddes owene heeste deere.   480
  Thy wyf and thou moote hange fer atwinne;
For that bitwixe yow shal be no sinne,
Namoore in looking than ther shal in deede,
This ordinance is seid. Go, God thee speede!
Tomorwe at night, whan men ben alle aslepe,   485
Into oure kneding-tubbes wol we crepe,
And sitten there, abiding Goddes grace.
Go now thy wey, I have no lenger space
To make of this no lenger sermoning.
Men seyn thus, "Sende the wise, and sey no thing:"   490
Thou art so wys, it needeth thee nat teche.
Go, save oure lyf, and that I the biseche.'
  This sely carpenter goth forth his wey.
Ful ofte he seide 'allas' and 'weylawey,'
And to his wyf he tolde his privetee,   495
And she was war, and knew it bet than he,
What al this queynte cast was for to seye.
But nathelees she ferde as she wolde deye,
And seide, 'Allas! go forth thy wey anon,
Help us to scape, or we been dede echon!   500
I am thy trewe, verray wedded wyf;
Go, deere spouse, and help to save oure lyf.'

- Lines 503–11 give rather a stirring account of John's state of mind. Discuss how this affects the reader, and decide who seems to be speaking these lines. Then summarise John's subsequent actions in lines 512 onwards, and consider whether that original (rather heroic) impression has been altered by what he actually does.
- What does the secrecy with which John goes about his preparations reveal about John's character and his response to Nicholas' story?
- It's important for a comic fabliau that before the action progresses all factual, physical details are made clear to the audience. Before the crucial night falls, take time to consider what information you can deduce about the whereabouts of all the characters, and how they are likely to behave, given the information you already possess. You may wish to present your ideas through a drawing of a cross-section of the carpenter's house.
- One theme that recurs frequently in *The Canterbury Tales* is the difference between appearance and reality. 'Hende' Nicholas, for instance, seems such a nice young man, discreet, musical, tidy, sweet-smelling, but when he was with Alison (lines 169–73) quite a different side of him was revealed. Make a note of other occasions within the tale when characters are revealed in a different light, as John is here.

503	**Lo, which a greet thing is affeccioun!** Behold how great is the power of love!	515	**heng hem ... privetee** hung them secretly in the rafters
505	**depe may impressioun be take** so deeply may a fear of imaginary disaster become	516	**his owene hand** by his own hand
		517	**stalkes** uprights
506	**quake** to shake	518	**balkes** rafters
507	**verraily that he may see** that he can actually see	519	**vitailled** provisioned [the sea-faring term]
508	**walwinge as the see** surging in like the sea	520	**jubbe** large jug
509	**drenchen** drown	521	**suffisinge right ynogh** fully sufficient
	hony deere sweet one	522	**er that he had maad al this array** before he made all these preparations
510	**maketh sory cheere** appears wretchedly miserable		
511	**siketh** sighs	524	**upon his nede** on an errand for him [A journey from Oxford to London would take about two days.]
	swogh groan		
514	**to his in** to his lodging house		

Frantic with worry at the thought of his beloved Alison perishing in a flood, John weeps and sighs;
then pulls himself together and bustles off to make preparations, storing three tubs secretly in the
roof, making rope ladders, getting in a stock of provisions, and sending his man and maidservant
to London.

Lo, which a greet thing is affeccioun!
Men may dyen of imaginacioun,
So depe may impressioun be take.   505
This sely carpenter biginneth quake;
Him thinketh verraily that he may see
Noees flood come walwinge as the see
To drenchen Alisoun, his hony deere.
He wepeth, weileth, maketh sory cheere;   510
He siketh with ful many a sory swogh;
He gooth and geteth him a kneding trogh,
And after that a tubbe and a kymelin,
And prively he sente hem to his in,
And heng hem in the roof in privetee.   515
    His owene hand he made laddres thre,
To climben by the ronges and the stalkes
Unto the tubbes hanginge in the balkes,
And hem vitailled, bothe trogh and tubbe,
With breed and chese, and good ale in a jubbe,   520
Suffisinge right ynogh as for a day.
But er that he hadde maad al this array,
He sente his knave, and eek his wenche also,
Upon his nede to London for to go.

- For Nicholas and Alison this is just a game to be played with mock solemnity until they can escape into John's bed. How does Chaucer successfully emphasise the humour of this stage of the farce?
- Look closely at lines 538–9: how far are we meant to sympathise with John here? And how does the author deliberately limit our sympathy?
- The irony with which Chaucer links the celebration of religious observances and the celebration of carnal pleasures is very obvious in lines 545–8. Religious ceremony and routine were essential parts of every person's life in the fourteenth century (see page 93). Chaucer suggests that for some at least it had very little spiritual significance.

525 **drow to night** night fell

526 **withoute candel-light** [no candle lit to show someone was at home]

527 **dressed alle thing** prepared everything

528 **up they clomben** up they climbed

529 **seten stille wel a furlong way** sat still and silent for as long as it would take to travel a furlong [about two minutes]

530 **'Now, *Pater noster*, clom!'** 'Now, say the Our Father and then hush!'

532 **seide his devocioun** said his prayers

533 **biddeth his preyere** made his own personal prayer

534 **Awaitinge on the reyn, if he it heere** waiting for the rain, to see if he could hear it

535 **wery bisynesse** sheer business [*i.e.* busy-ness – he had had a very tiring day]

537 **corfew- time** curfew time [About 8 p.m. – from the French *couvre feu*, when a bell was rung to indicate that workmen's fires and lights were to be extinguished. Any later was considered too dark to produce good work.]

538–9 **For travaille ... his heed mislay** He groaned most bitterly because of spiritual wretchedness, and what is more he snored, because his head lay lopsidedly

543 **Ther as the carpenter is wont to lie** right there where the carpenter usually lay [an emphasis on the boldness of the cuckoldry; note the speed with which the encounter is accomplished and described – after all the elaborate preparation]

544 **Ther was the revel and the melodie** That's where the song and dance took place

546 **In bisynesse of mirth and of solas** Fully engrossed in enjoyment and mutual delight

547 **belle of laudes** [The bell for lauds would ring around 3 a.m. – at this time religious clerks would celebrate the first service of the church day. Both Nicholas and Absolon are engaged in very different diversions.]

548 **freres in the chauncel gonne singe** friars went to sing in the chancel [Again music punctuates the action – ironically here.]

*By Monday night all is arranged according to plan, the three settle quietly in their respective tubs.
Nicholas calls for silence after prayer. The carpenter listens for rain, but, exhausted, soon sleeps,
snoring heavily. Nicholas and Alison creep down their ladders and enjoy themselves in the
carpenter's bed.*

And on the Monday, whan it drow to night, 525
He shette his dore withoute candel-light,
And dressed alle thing as it sholde be.
And shortly, up they clomben alle thre:
They seten stille wel a furlong way.
 'Now, *Pater-noster*, clom!' seide Nicholay, 530
And 'clom,' quod John, and 'clom' seide Alisoun.
This carpenter seide his devocioun,
And stille he sit, and biddeth his preyere,
Awaitinge on the reyn, if he it heere.
 The dede sleep, for wery bisynesse, 535
Fil on this carpenter right, as I gesse,
Aboute corfew-time, or litel moore;
For travaille of his goost he groneth soore,
And eft he routeth, for his heed mislay.
Doun of the laddre stalketh Nicholay, 540
And Alisoun ful softe adoun she spedde;
Withouten wordes mo they goon to bedde,
Ther as the carpenter is wont to lie.
Ther was the revel and the melodie;
And thus lith Alison and Nicholas, 545
In bisynesse of mirthe and of solas,
Til that the belle of laudes gan to ringe,
And freres in the chauncel gonne singe.

*'And thus lith Alison and Nicholas,
In bisynesse of mirthe and of solas'*

Chaucer's skilled storytelling becomes increasingly apparent as the action reaches its climax. All the information we need to clarify the situation has already been given to us. We know why John has not been seen since Saturday, just as we know what Absolon will decide to do, and who exactly is in the bedroom he will serenade. We know too that the carpenter, fast asleep in his tub, is too exhausted to be woken by any singing. All that remains is to consider the characters of Nicholas, Alison and Absolon and to decide how the plot will develop.

• Look at the speech given to the anonymous monk in lines 556–62. Is it possible to deduce from this something of his character?
• Look at the chance remark on line 553, and make notes, as the tale progresses, on the way in which chance or fortune alters the outcome, in spite of Nicholas' elaborate planning.

549 **amorous** lovesick

550 **wo bigon** woebegone, wretched

552 **him to disporte and pleye** to pass the time, enjoy himself

553 **axed upon cas a cloisterer** by chance asked one of the monks

554 **ful prively** secretly

555 **drough him aparte** took him aside [maybe guessing the reason for his interest]

556 **noot** don't know [*abbrev*: 'ne woot']

556–7 **I saugh ... Saterday** I haven't seen him here at work since Saturday

557 **I trowe** I guess

559 **he is wont** he is accustomed to

560 **dwellen at the grange** stay at the grange [The outlying farm or monastic house from where the carpenter would collect timber for his work on the abbey at Osney.]

561 **or elles ... certein** or else he must definitely be at his own house

562 **soothly** truly

563 **light** lighthearted

565 **sikirly** truly
nat stiringe not moving about

566 **sin day bigan to springe** since daybreak [Poor John has been too busy secretly fixing his tubs.]

567 **So moot I thrive** As I live and breathe!

569 **stant ful low upon his boures wal** set low down on his bedroom wall [The position is important.]

Absolon was at Osney on that Monday; not seeing John there, he asked after him. He learnt that he had not been seen since Saturday, and was probably away from home. Joyfully he sees this as an opportunity to serenade Alison undisturbed.

This parissh clerk, this amorous Absolon,
That is for love alwey so wo bigon,   550
Upon the Monday was at Oseneye
With compaignie, him to disporte and pleye,
And axed upon cas a cloisterer
Ful prively after John the carpenter,
And he drough him apart out of the chirche,   555
And seide, 'I noot, I saugh him heere nat wirche
Sin Saterday; I trowe that he be went
For timber, ther oure abbot hath him sent;
For he is wont for timber for to go,
And dwellen at the grange a day or two;   560
Or elles he is at his hous, certein.
Where that he be, I kan nat soothly seyn.'
This Absolon ful joly was and light,
And thoghte, 'Now is time to wake al night;
For sikirly I saugh him nat stiringe   565
Aboute his dore, sin day bigan to springe.
So moot I thrive, I shal, at cokkes crowe,
Ful prively knokken at his windowe
That stant ful lowe upon his boures wal.

*'he is wont for timber for to go,
And dwellen at the grange a day or two'*

- Can't you just imagine Absolon? How do the details Chaucer gives us here make him sound absurd, affected, over-optimistic, and undoubtedly a failure?
- What do you think about the way both Absolon and John look for signs and portents to reveal the future? On the other hand, Nicholas cynically exploits superstitious beliefs, clearly doesn't believe his own fortune-telling, and relies on his wits. Is his hard-headed scepticism more admirable than the beliefs of John and Absolon?
- Write a description of a young man of today preparing for an opportunity to win the girl of his dreams. Is it possible to suggest to your audience, as Chaucer does with Absolon, that he is likely to fail in his endeavours?

571 **yet I shalle nat misse** I can't fail this time

572 **at the leeste wey** at the very least

573 **Som maner confort** some sort of reward [He feels he's worked very hard at this wooing.]

574 **mouth hath icched** [Superstition still holds that itching palms suggest money on the way.]

576 **me mette eek I was at a feeste** I also dreamt I was at a feast [He will receive a reward on the mouth he doesn't expect.]

578 **pleye** make love [Chaucer deliberately uses a childish word here.]

580 **Up rist** up rose

581 **him arraieth gay, at point-devis** dressed himself with great care and attention

582 **cheweth greyn and licoris** he chewed grain and liquorice [Again the mouth and sweet breath are mentioned, as in lines 153–4.]

583 **er he hadde kembd his heer** before he combed his hair [He's very proud of his hair; see lines 206–8.]

584 **a trewe-love he beer** he slipped a sprig of herb-paris [for luck in love, perhaps?]

585 **therby wende he to ben gracious** by doing these things he thought he'd prove irresistible

586 **rometh** set off

587 **stille he stant** he stood silently

shot-windowe [Chaucer reminds us again it is a window which opens on a hinge.]

588 **Unto his brest it raughte** it reached just to his chest [another important reminder]

589 **cougheth with a semy soun** softly and genteelly cleared his throat

Absolon has had signs and dreams which seem to promise him that he will get a kiss from Alison, at the very least. Dressed to kill, having sweetened his breath and combed his hair, he settles himself beneath the window of the carpenter's house, and prepares to sing …

To Alison now wol I tellen al   570
My love-longinge, for yet I shal nat misse
That at the leeste wey I shal hire kisse.
Som maner confort shal I have, parfay.
My mouth hath icched al this longe day;
That is a signe of kissing atte leeste.   575
Al night me mette eek I was at a feeste.
Therfore I wol go slepe an houre or tweye,
And al the night thane wol I wake and pleye.'
   Whan that the firste cok hath crowe, anon
Up rist this joly lovere Absolon,   580
And him arraieth gay, at point-devis.
But first he cheweth greyn and licoris,
To smellen sweete, er he hadde kembd his heer.
Under his tonge a trewe-love he beer,
For therby wende he to ben gracious.   585
He rometh to the carpenteres hous,
And stille he stant under the shot-windowe—
Unto his brest it raughte, it was so lowe—
And softe he cougheth with a semy soun:
'What do ye, hony-comb, sweete Alisoun,   590

'Al night me mette eek I was at a feeste'

65

- Working with a partner, read (or sing) Absolon's lament and Alison's reply, attempting to capture the tone and attitude of both characters. How might a modern suitor serenade his beloved?
- Look closely at the words and tone of Absolon's song (lines 590–9). There are echoes of serenades from courtly love romances, and also reminders of the biblical Song of Solomon (turtle doves, cinnamon). Nevertheless, he seems unable to sustain a truly tender and beautiful mood. Where does he go wrong? (For example, look at line 596.)
- Absolon strives yet again to behave and sound like a courtly squire; even if he had succeeded in creating the right atmosphere, how does Alison manage to destroy it in lines 600–5?
- Both Nicholas (lines 168–85) and Absolon were initially rejected by Alison. How does their approach to rejection differ?

591 **faire brid, my sweete cinamome** my pretty bird, my sweet cinnamon

592 **lemman myn** my beloved

593 **Wel litel thinken ye** how little concern you have for

594 **I swete ther I go** I sweat wherever I walk

595 **swelte** swelter

596 **moorne** yearn
as dooth a lamb after the tete like a lamb for its mother's teat [Remember his pride in his curly hair.]

597 **ywis** you know

598 **lik a turtel trewe is my moorninge** my anguish is like that of the faithful turtle dove

599 **I may ete ... a maide** I can't eat any more than a young girl

600 **Jakke fool** stupid idiot [a popular term of abuse and contempt]

601 **As help me ... com pa me** I swear you'll get no 'come and kiss me' here

602 **elles I were to blame** or else I would be at fault [She implies she's speaking of her husband.]

603 **Wel bet than thee** a far better man than you [Is she referring to her husband here?]

604 **I wol caste a ston** I'll throw a stone at you

605 **a twenty devel wey** in the name of twenty devils

606 **weylawey** woe is me

607 **so ivel biset** so cruelly denied

608 **sin it may be no bet** since that's the best I can hope for

610 **Wiltow thanne** will you [*abbrev.* 'wilt thou'] then

611 **certes** truly, certainly

612 **anon** straight away

Absolon's song fails to impress Alison, who tells him she loves another, and that he should go away and let her sleep. But when he says he'll leave if she gives him a kiss first, she agrees to come to the window.

My faire brid, my sweete cinamome?
Awaketh, lemman myn, and speketh to me!
Wel litel thinken ye upon my wo,
That for youre love I swete ther I go.
No wonder is thogh that I swelte and swete;   595
I moorne as dooth a lamb after the tete.
Ywis, lemman, I have swich love-longinge,
That lik a turtel trewe is my moorninge.
I may nat ete na moore than a maide.'
    'Go fro the window, Jakke fool,' she saide;   600
'As help me God, it wol nat be "com pa me".
I love another—and elles I were to blame—
Wel bet than thee, by Jhesu, Absolon.
Go forth thy way, or I wol caste a ston,
And lat me slepe, a twenty devel wey!'   605
    'Allas,' quod Absolon, 'and weylawey,
That trewe love was evere so ivel biset!
Thanne kisse me, sin it may be no bet,
For Jhesus love, and for the love of me.'
    'Wiltow thanne go thy wey therwith?' quod she.   610
    'Ye, certes, lemman,' quod this Absolon.
    'Thanne make thee redy,' quod she, 'I come anon.'

- Working with a partner, read aloud Absolon's speech (lines 616–18) and Alison's (lines 620–1) in such a way that the contrast between them is clearly revealed. Make a note of the way in which Absolon's actions and language show that his view of himself and his pursuit of Alison is quite different from hers. Notice the differing rhythm and vocabulary Chaucer uses to emphasise this contrast in these lines.
- Although there is little description at this point, how does Chaucer wring the maximum humour out of the situation through the way in which he tells the joke?

613   **stille** softly

614   **hust** keep quiet

       laughen al thy fille have a good laugh

616   **I am a lord at alle degrees** I am a lord in every way [He still sees himself as a gallant, courtly lover.]

617   **I hope ther cometh moore** I hope there'll be more to follow

618   **Lemman, thy grace, and sweete brid, thyn oore!** Your courtesy, my beloved, and, sweet bird, your grace and favour!

620–1   **Have do, quod she ... thee espie** Have done, come on and get it over with before the neighbours see you

623   **as pich or as the cole** as pitch or coal

625   **him fil no bet ne wers** no better nor worse happened to him [*i.e.* this is exactly what happened]

627   **ful savoury** with great relish

       er he were war before he was aware

628   **Abak he stirte** back he jumped

       it was amis something wasn't quite right

629   **wel he wiste** he well knew

       berd beard

630   **long yherd** long-haired, shaggy

631   **what have I do?** what have I done?

632   **clapte the window to** slammed the window shut

633   **a sory pas** in a most dreadful state

Alison promises Nicholas a laugh. Absolon kneels by the window and puckers up for a kiss; she sticks out her bare bottom and Absolon kisses that, to his horror. With a giggle she shuts the window.

And unto Nicholas she seide stille,
  'Now hust, and thou shalt laughen al thy fille.'
  This Absolon doun sette him on his knees   615
And seide, 'I am a lord at alle degrees;
For after this I hope ther cometh moore.
Lemman, thy grace, and sweete brid, thyn oore!'
  The window she undoth, and that in haste.
'Have do,' quod she, 'com of, and speed the faste,   620
Lest that oure neighebores thee espie.'
  This Absolon gan wipe his mouth ful drie.
Derk was the night as pich, or as the cole,
And at the window out she putte hir hole,
And Absolon, him fil no bet ne wers,   625
But with his mouth he kiste hir naked ers
Ful savourly, er he were war of this.
Abak he stirte, and thoughte it was amis,
For wel he wiste a womman hath no berd.
He felte a thing al rough and long yherd,   630
And seide, 'Fy! allas! what have I do?'
  'Tehee!' quod she, and clapte the window to,
And Absolon gooth forth a sory pas.

- Look again at Absolon's preparations for wooing Alison (lines 570–90), the importance of having sweet breath, his dream of kisses, his honeyed words, and notice how Chaucer continues to stress descriptions of his mouth, in order to draw ironic attention to his reaction.
- Chaucer likens Absolon to a beaten child (line 651); where have you noticed any earlier examples of childishness in him?
- Love for Alison very quickly turns to hate after she plays her trick. Would you say Chaucer intended his audience to believe Absolon was ever deeply in love? Is there any indication that any character in this tale feels emotion at a deeper level? Would deep emotional responses be appropriate in a tale of this type?
- Consider Nicholas' reaction to Alison's joke. What does it add to his characterisation?

634   **a berd** [Nicholas seems to guess that Absolon thought at first he'd kissed a beard – Absolon may even have spoken his thoughts aloud.]

635   **By ... faire and weel** by the body of Christ this was a magnificent trick to play

636   **every deel** every word

637   **he gan** he began

638   **quite** pay [you] back

639   **Who** [who is it now that ...?]
       froteth scrubs

640   **chippes** wood shavings

642–4   **My soul bitake I unto Sathanas ... for to be** May I pledge my soul to the devil if I wouldn't rather get my revenge for this insult than be the owner of this whole town

645   **allas I ne hadde ybleynt** how distressing that I didn't avoid it [her bottom, presumably]

646   **al yqueynt** totally quenched

648   **he sette nat a kers** he cared nothing at all for them

649   **heeled of his maladie** cured of his sickness [In courtly romances love is often regarded as a sickness.]

650   **paramours** lovers
       gan deffie began to cast off, reject

651   **that is ybete** that is beaten

Whilst Nicholas guffaws at the good trick, Absolon furiously seeks revenge, quite cured of his love
for Alison, or, indeed, for anyone.

'A berd! a berd!' quod hende Nicholas,
'By Goddes corpus, this goth faire and weel.'   635
    This sely Absolon herde every deel,
And on his lippe he gan for anger bite,
And to himself he seide, 'I shal thee quite.'
    Who rubbeth now, who froteth now his lippes
With dust, with sond, with straw, with clooth, with chippes, 640
But Absolon, that seith ful ofte, 'Allas!
My soule bitake I unto Sathanas,
But me were levere than al this toun,' quod he,
'Of this despit awroken for to be.
Allas,' quod he, 'allas, I ne hadde ybleynt!'   645
His hoote love was coold and al yqueynt;
For fro that time that he hadde kist hir ers,
Of paramours he sette nat a kers;
For he was heeled of his maladie.
Ful ofte paramours he gan deffie,   650
And weep as dooth a child that is ybete.

- The come-uppance of the lovesick parish clerk might have seemed a good place to end this tale, but there is a further unexpected twist to events. When you have read the final section, decide what would have been lost if it had been omitted.
- The conversation with Gervais is informative in a number of ways. Not only do we learn something of Gervais' character, but we can also deduce facts about Absolon's reputation in Oxford and his frame of mind. Not least we are given a hint that something devilish will soon take place. How does Chaucer convey all this information in these few lines?

652	**a softe paas** quietly	
653	**cleped daun Gerveys** called [named] Master Gervais	
654	**smithed plough harneys** hammered ploughing gear [Smiths were often required to work very early in the morning on tools that were needed later that day.]	
655	**sharpeth shaar and kultour** sharpened ploughshare and coulter [The coulter is the knife on a plough that cuts the earth into furrows; the mould-board, or share, turns the cut earth to one side.]	
656	**al esily** gently	
657	**undo** open up	
658	**artow** art thou [are you]	
660	**rathe** early	
	benedicitee! God bless us!	
661	**What eyleth yow** what's the matter?	
	Som gey gerl, God it woot By God I expect it's some lively young girl	
662	**upon the viritoot** up and about and full of beans [The smith hints	

that sexual adventures have persuaded Absolon to be up and about so early in the morning.]

663	**Seinte Note** St Neot [a local Saxon saint]	
664–5	**ne roghte nat ... he yaf** didn't care a jot for all this joking; he didn't stoop to reply	
666	**hadde moore tow on his distaf** [tow is the unspun wool or flax that is turned into yarn on a distaff – in other words he had more business in hand]	
668	**hoote kultour in the chimenee** hot coulter in the hearth	
669	**lene** lend	
	I have therwith to doone there's something I want to do with it	
671–2	**were it ... alle untold** even if it were gold, or a sack of uncounted gold coins	
673	**Cristes foo!** Christ's foe! [*i.e.* the devil]	
675	**be as be may** never you mind	
677	**by the colde stele** by the unheated part of the metal	

Absolon quietly crosses the street to the forge, where he asks the blacksmith if he can borrow a knife he is sharpening. Ignoring the smith's curiosity and witticisms, Absolon takes the hot knife from the fireplace, and says he'll explain why he needed it at a later date.

A softe paas he wente over the strete
Until a smith men cleped daun Gerveys,
That in his forge smithed plough harneys;
He sharpeth shaar and kultour bisily.   655
This Absolon knokketh al esily,
And seide, 'Undo, Gerveys, and that anon.'
   'What, who artow?' 'It am I, Absolon.'
   'What, Absolon! for Cristes sweete tree,
Why rise ye so rathe? ey, *benedicitee*!   660
What eyleth yow? Som gay gerl, God it woot,
Hath broght yow thus upon the viritoot.
By Seinte Note, ye woot wel what I mene.'
   This Absolon ne roghte nat a bene
Of al his pley; no word again he yaf;   665
He hadde moore tow on his distaf
Than Gerveys knew, and seide, 'Freend so deere,
That hoote kultour in the chimenee heere,
As lene it me, I have therwith to doone,
And I wol bringe it thee again ful soone.'   670
   Gerveys answerde, 'Certes, were it gold,
Or in a poke nobles alle untold,
Thou sholdest have, as I am trewe smith.
Ey, Cristes foo! what wol ye do therwith?'
   'Therof,' quod Absolon, 'be as be may.   675
I shal wel telle it thee to-morwe day'—
And caughte the kultour by the colde stele.

'He sharpeth shaar and kultour bisily' (Both ploughshare and cultour are clearly visible here.)

- In what way is Nicholas' attempt to improve the joke more or less funny than Alison's original action? Discuss whether it seems in keeping with what Chaucer has told us of his character that he should wish to go one step further.
- Working with a partner, one supporting Nicholas, the other Absolon, discuss whether we are intended to feel sorry for Absolon at any stage in the proceedings, or for Nicholas, given that we know exactly what Absolon is holding in his hand.
- In groups of four give a reading of the dialogue between Absolon and Alison (lines 680–7), two people speaking the actual words, two explaining, at the end of each sentence, what each character is really thinking.

680   **therwithal** in addition

681   **right as he dide er** just as he did before

683   **I warante it a theef** I reckon it's a thief

685   **deereling** darling [Absolon is capable of making sweet speeches whether he means them or not.]

686   **I have thee broght a ring** I have a ring for you [Lines 142–58 suggested Alison's love of finery.]

687   **My mooder yaf it me, so God me save** I swear by God my mother gave it to me

688   **wel ygrave** finely engraved

691   **he wolde amenden al the jape** enhance the original joke

692   **kisse his ers er that he scape** kiss his arse before he got away

693   **up the windowe dide he hastily** he quickly threw open the window

695   **haunche-bon** hip bone

696   **therwith** just then

697   **noot nat** I don't know

Once more Absolon returns to the window, and tells Alison that he'll give her a gold ring in return for another kiss. Thinking he can improve on the joke still further, Nicholas thrusts his backside out of the window.

Ful softe out at the dore he gan to stele,
And wente unto the carpenteris wal.
He cogheth first, and knokketh therwithal   680
Upon the windowe, right as he dide er.
   This Alison answerde, 'Who is ther
That knokketh so? I warante it a theef.'
   'Why, nay,' quod he, 'God woot, my sweete leef,
I am thyn Absolon, my deereling.   685
Of gold,' quod he, 'I have thee broght a ring.
My mooder yaf it me, so God me save;
Ful fyn it is, and therto wel ygrave.
This wol I yeve thee, if thou me kisse.'
   This Nicholas was risen for to pisse,   690
And thoughte he wolde amenden al the jape;
He sholde kisse his ers er that he scape.
And up the windowe dide he hastily,
And out his ers he putteth prively
Over the buttok, to the haunche-bon;   695
And therwith spak this clerk, this Absolon,
'Spek, sweete brid, I noot nat where thou art.'

- Present these lines as a dramatic reading (with sound effects) in order to appreciate the vitality of the writing. Take particular note of where and how the pace of the reading should alter. What techniques can you use to show that the actions happen almost simultaneously, without losing the important explanatory details?
- Prepare timelines tracing the two sets of events – the deception of John by Nicholas and the attempted wooing by Absolon of Alison, showing clearly how each develops, from the moment Nicholas declares his desire for Alison, on one hand, and Absolon makes eyes at her in church on the other. Consider Chaucer's skill as a storyteller at the point where the two chains of events inevitably coincide.
- What techniques does Chaucer employ to achieve the sudden flurry of noise and movement after the quiet, secretive preparations of the revengeful Absolon previously described? Look carefully at vocabulary, rhythm and sentence structure.
- Summarise the injuries all three men have endured in some way by the end of this section. How far does the audience feel sympathetic towards all or any of them? Should there be sympathy for Alison?

698	**leet fle** lets out	706	**as he were wood** as if he were mad
699	**thonder-dent** clap of thunder [an appropriate simile in the circumstances]		**gan** began
		708	**out of his slomber sterte** started out of his sleep
700	**with the strook he was almoost yblent** he was almost blinded by the blast	709	**herde oon** heard someone
		711	**withouten wordes mo** without another word
701	**and he was redy with his iren hoot** and he [Absolon] was waiting with his hot iron [So clearly can we visualise events there is no confusion for the audience in the use of 'he' again here.]	712	**smoot the corde atwo** split the rope in two
		713	**doun gooth al** down came the lot
		713–14	**he foond ... to the celle** he found no time to get to grips with either the bread or the ale until he hit the ground [Eating and drinking arrangements are given respectful attention – appropriately so in a tale supposedly told by a trencherman like the Miller. Poor John has no chance to enjoy the tasty provisions he collected so assiduously the day before.]
702	**amidde the ers** slap in the middle of his backside		
703	**Of gooth the skin** the skin is burnt off		
	hande-brede aboute a patch as big as a hand		
704	**brende so his toute** burnt his behind so badly		
705	**smert** pain	715	**aswowne** unconscious
	wende believed		

Just as Nicholas lets out a huge fart Absolon brands him with the hot iron. Nicholas' agonised cry
for water at last awakes John, who thinks this is the sign the flood has arrived, chops his retaining
rope in two, and crashes to the ground.

   This Nicholas anon leet fle a fart,
As greet as it had been a thonder-dent,
That with the strook he was almoost yblent;   700
And he was redy with his iren hoot,
And Nicholas amidde the ers he smoot.
   Of gooth the skin an hande-brede aboute,
The hoote kultour brende so his toute,
And for the smert he wende for to die.   705
As he were wood, for wo he gan to crie,
'Help! water! water! help, for Goddes herte!'
   This carpenter out of his slomber sterte,
And herde oon crien 'water' as he were wood,
And thoughte, 'Allas, now comth Nowelis flood!'   710
He sit him up withouten wordes mo,
And with his ax he smoot the corde atwo,
And doun gooth al; he foond neither to selle,
Ne breed ne ale, til he cam to the celle
Upon the floor, and ther aswowne he lay.   715

- The beauty of Nicholas' plan becomes completely clear at this point. Summarise the main points of his plan, and then discuss with a partner how effectively he achieves his aim of sleeping with Alison whilst maintaining his reputation for being 'hende' and successfully avoiding the wrath of his landlord.
- Does Nicholas deserve his injury?
- Discuss Alison's treatment of her husband. Are her actions in keeping with her character?

716	**stirte** leapt, jumped
717	**criden 'out' and 'harrow'** cried 'help' and 'save us'
718	**both smale and grete** both rich and poor
719	**In ronnen for to gauren** came running up to stare at
721	**with the fal he brosten hadde his arm** in the fall he had broken his arm [Quite a long fall – although Nicholas rents an upstairs room, it seems that at least one part of the carpenter's house has no intervening upper storey, and John has fallen from the rafters to the ground floor, allowing the townsfolk a good view of him.]
722	**stonde he moste unto his owene harm** he must take responsibility for his own injury [*i.e.* no-one is going to feel sorry for him]

723–4	**he was anon … and Alisoun** he was immediately interrupted and contradicted by that pleasant young man Nicholas and by Alison [Perhaps nowhere does the word 'hende' have a crueller twist than here.]
725	**wood** mad
726	**agast so** so terrified
727	**Thurgh fantasie** because of some delusion
	of his vanitee in his folly
730	**he preyed hem** he begged them [*i.e.* Nicholas and Alison]
731	*par compaignie* for company [The French phrase gives an absurd social distinction to the account.]

Nicholas and Alison rush into the street, crying out for help. A small crowd gathers to look at the injured man, John, but his explanations are cut short by his wife and lodger, who tell people he is mad, and is possessed of a strange delusion about Noah's flood.

Up stirte hire Alison and Nicholay,
And criden 'out' and 'harrow' in the strete.
The neighebores, bothe smale and grete,
In ronnen for to gauren on this man,
That yet aswowne lay, bothe pale and wan,   720
For with the fal he brosten hadde his arm.
But stonde he moste unto his owene harm;
For whan he spak, he was anon bore doun
With hende Nicholas and Alisoun.
They tolden every man that he was wood,   725
He was agast so of Nowelis flood
Thurgh fantasie, that of his vanitee
He hadde yboght him kneding tubbes thre,
And hadde hem hanged in the roof above;
And that he preyed hem, for Goddes love,   730
To sitten in the roof, *par compaignie.*

- Summarise the way in which John, Nicholas, Absolon and Alison have been punished. Does it seem to you that justice has been equally meted out to all four? And does this matter, given that this is a fabliau, and not intended to be taken seriously?
- The last five lines (lines 742–6) certainly sound as if they might well be spoken by a drunken Miller. How much of the earlier parts of the tale are narrated in his voice?
- Have you enjoyed this tale? Did the humour outweigh the vulgarity?
- Which has proved to be the best way to produce a desired effect in this tale – clever use of words by educated men, or straightforward, physical action?

732 **fantasie** delusion

733 **they kiken and they cape** they peered and gaped

734 **turned al his harm unto a jape** turned all the harm that had come to him into a joke

735–6 **what so that ... his reson herde** whatever the carpenter might say it did no good, for no-one listened to him

737 **othes grete** great declarations

so sworne adoun sworn or shouted down

738 **holde** considered

739 **every clerk anonright heeld with oother** every clerk immediately sided with another [*i.e.* Nicholas; a hint here that, even if anyone suspected John had been tricked, he would not side with a townsman against a scholar]

740 **leeve brother** dear brother, fellow clerk

741 **wight** person

stryf trouble, predicament

742 **swived** sexually satisfied

743 **for al his keping** in spite of his attempts to keep her under his control

744 **nether ye** bottom

745 **in the towte** on his rump

746 **al the rowte** all this company [With these words we are abruptly returned to the imaginary group of pilgrims, Chaucer's fictional audience.]

People laughed and gaped up at the rafters; no-one listened to the carpenter's explanation – the whole town thought him mad. And so the carpenter's wife had a fling despite her jealous husband, Absolon gets kissed and Nicholas gets burnt. The tale is over.

    The folk gan laughen at his fantasie;
Into the roof they kiken and they cape,
And turned al his harm unto a jape.
For what so that this carpenter answerde,   735
It was for noght, no man his reson herde.
With othes grete he was so sworn adoun
That he was holde wood in al the toun;
For every clerk anonright heeld with oother.
They seide, 'The man is wood, my leeve brother';   740
And every wight gan laughen at this stryf.
    Thus swived was this carpenteris wyf,
For al his keping and his jalousie;
And Absolon hath kist hir nether ye;
And Nicholas is scalded in the towte.   745
This tale is doon, and God save al the rowte!

'And turned al his harm unto a jape'

Comparing the Miller's Tale with the Knight's Tale: the fabliau and the courtly romance

Chaucer chooses to begin his *Canterbury Tales* with masterly examples of two very dissimilar literary genres. So different is the courtly romance, told by the Knight, from the fabliau, told by the Miller, that it comes as something of a surprise to discover how similar are the themes of the two tales. Chaucer is not simply flexing his creative muscles here – he is indicating that the scope of *The Canterbury Tales* reaches from one extreme to the other. The variety of tales he allocates to his miscellany of characters will convey many different attitudes to life and society.

ROMANCES AND FABLIAUX

Romances had long been a very popular form of fiction in medieval literature. Essentially a romance was concerned with the actions of courtly, noble characters. Most were also love stories; frequently they described chivalrous adventures. They were likely to offer a strongly moral stance, and reminders of the highest ideals towards which mankind should aim. Fabliaux were also very popular. These essentially comical stories were concerned with contemporary life, and with all those aspects of human behaviour that dismiss ideals and moral scruples as mere irrelevances. Fabliaux and romances were well liked by similar audiences. By introducing his collection of stories in this manner Chaucer is illustrating his skill as a hugely varied writer. Some of the more obvious contrasts between fabliaux and romances are explained below.

A courtly image of a romantic knight and his lady

COMPARING THE TWO TALES

Theme The contrast between the two tales is made even more illuminating by the fact that both deal with a love triangle. In the Knight's Tale two young knights, Palamon and Arcite, boon companions and royally born, are imprisoned after a battle in which they had been defeated. They see a beautiful maiden from their cell window, and imediately both fall in love with her, becoming rivals for her love (though neither has even spoken to her). Their escape and subsequent adventures form the substance of this long tale, which culminates in a fierce and gallant tournament, when many knights are killed or seriously wounded in the names of honour, chivalry and love. Arcite wins the tournament, and the girl, but at the last moment the god Saturn intervenes, causing him to be thrown from his horse. He dies in agony, and Emily becomes the bride of Palamon. Both young men have behaved with impeccable good taste throughout the proceedings.

In the Miller's Tale idealised love for a remote and unattainable heroine is replaced by a contest to bed an attractive young woman, who is already married to an older husband, but nevertheless quite prepared to enter into a liaison with some enthusiasm. Moral scruples have no place in events described here; knockabout comedy is the key to all the action, and broken arms, burnt flesh and hurt pride are all equally cause for laughter. Yearning for love causes anguish and pain in the courtly romance – hunger for sex causes anguish and pain of a very different kind to Alison's admirers.

Setting It was customary to set romances in the distant past, and in a distant country. The Knight's Tale is set in Athens, during the reign of Duke Theseus. The gods and goddesses of classical mythology – Saturn, Venus and Mars - take an active part in events.

The Miller's Tale, on the other hand, has all the immediacy of a daily paper. It is set in contemporary Oxford, a town probably familiar to many of Chaucer's original audience. The sights and sounds of the town, the bustle and everyday activities of the ordinary inhabitants, form the lively and essential background to events.

Language and style Chaucer wrote the tale of Palamon and Arcite some time before he developed the idea of *The Canterbury Tales*. Much longer than any of the other tales, it was derived from a story of Boccaccio's, and is influenced by Chaucer's admiration for the philosophy of Boethius. The structure is complicated; there are long descriptive passages, debates concerning such diverse matters as the essence of war, the influence of Providence in guiding the affairs of men, the pain of love. The language abounds in abstract concepts: pity, honour, loyalty, mercy, justice. The tone is thoughtful, ruminative, melancholic. Ideas and ideals are more important than characters.

By contrast the Miller's Tale is one of the shortest in the series. There is plenty of dialogue, but spats and arguments, rather than debates. The audience is constantly made aware of the everyday world of a small town: the domestic animals, colts, sheep, geese, ducks; the sounds from a blacksmith's forge, and the church bells; the

A town scene from the fourteenth century

barns, the kitchen utensils, the windows and doors of houses. Vivid realisation of even the most minor characters involved in the plot also adds notably to the liveliness of the tale. The physical surroundings relating to events are most carefully revealed to the audience so that the speedy development of events that provide the climax of the plot can be fully realised without need for further description or explanation. The language is informal, conversational, and concerned with what we experience with our five senses, rather than any spiritual or cerebral impulses.

Characters The two knights, Palamon and Arcite, in the first tale, are barely distinguishable from one another, being equally noble, brave and suffering from similar pangs of despairing love. By contrast we have a very clear idea of the differing personalities of Nicholas and Absolon, from the careful way in which both are introduced at the beginning of the Miller's Tale, and through their subsequent behaviour. Although many fabliaux lacked much clear characterisation, this tale owes a great deal of its exuberance to the vivid picture of those involved, the rival clerks and subsequently John, the old husband. However, the contrast between the Knight's and Miller's tales is perhaps most clearly noticeable in the manner of portraying the two women – Emily and Alison. Emily, sister of Queen Hippolyta, is an appropriate heroine for a romance: we are told she is fairer than a lily; her complexion rivals that of the roses she gathers to make a garland for her golden hair; she is seen in a garden, on an early May morning, and she sings, of course, like an angel. She is presented as the standard stereotype of the beautiful heroine. We scarcely hear her speak, nor does she ever give any indication of affection for either suitor. She remains throughout the tale an unattainable idealised image of perfect womanhood, but she is never portrayed as a real person. Alison, the carpenter's wife, is one of Chaucer's great female characters. She could not be more different. The formalities of the conventional description of a heroine have been swept aside, and it seems that this eighteen-year old beauty with all her faults and fascination is as vividly recognisable now as she was six hundred years ago.

84

Chaucer's pilgrims

In order of appearance:

The Knight	brave, devout and unassuming – the perfect gentleman
The Squire	in training to follow in the footsteps of his father, the knight, a fine and fashionable young man, and madly in love
The Yeoman	the knight's only servant, a skilled bowman and forester
The Prioress	a most ladylike head of a nunnery; she takes great pains with her appearance and manners; she loves animals. She is accompanied by another nun and three priests, the nun and one priest also telling tales
The Monk	fine and prosperous looking, well-mounted; he loves hunting
The Friar	cheerful and sociable, he is skilled at obtaining alms from those he visits, particularly the ladies
The Merchant	rather secretive; his main interest is commerce
The Clerk	thin and shabby, his passion is scholarship; he spends all he has on books
The Sergeant at Law	a judge at the assize courts; one of the few pilgrims about whom Chaucer says very little
The Franklin	a wealthy and hospitable landowner and a JP; but not a member of the aristocracy

The Canterbury pilgrims leaving the Tabard Inn at Southwark

The Five Guildsmen	although they pursue different crafts or trades, they belong to the same social guild – rather self-important townsfolk
The Cook	he has been brought along to provide meals for the guildsmen; although he is a versatile cook, Chaucer suggests his personal hygiene could be improved
The Shipman	a weather-beaten master mariner
The Doctor of Physic	finely dressed and a skilled medical practitioner; he is an expert in astrology and natural magic; he loves gold
The Wife of Bath	skilled at weaving; her chief claim to fame is her five husbands
The Parson	the only truly devout churchman in Chaucer's group; he avoids all the tricks unscrupulous clerics used to get rich, and spends his care and energy on his parishioners
The Ploughman	the parson's brother and, like him, a simple, honest hard-working man
The Miller	tough, ugly, and a cheat
The Manciple	responsible for organising the provisions for the lawyers in one of the Inns of Court – clearly a plum job for a clever man
The Reeve	unsociable, but able; the estate manager of a young nobleman
The Summoner	an official of a church court; corrupt, lewd and offensive
The Pardoner	another unpleasant churchman – he earns money by selling 'pardons' from Rome, and by letting simple folk see the fake holy relics he carries
The Host	the genial landlord of 'The Tabard', who accompanies them on the pilgrimage, and organises the storytelling
Geoffrey Chaucer	he depicts himself as rather shy and unassuming

They are later joined by another storyteller – **The Canon's Yeoman**, a servant whose tale betrays his master's obsessive interest in alchemy.

Modern pilgrims

Pilgrims and pilgrimages

Pilgrimages are journeys made to sacred places, usually as acts of religious devotion. They became increasingly popular during the twelfth and thirteenth centuries, at the time when threats to the Christian world from infidels and heathens, as Chaucer would have called them, reached their height. The passion to defend and reaffirm the power of the Christian church manifested itself in Crusades to the Holy Land, and an upsurge in religious fervour. Shrines were established in many European countries in places of great religious significance. In England, Canterbury Cathedral was the site of the assassination of Archbishop Becket; Walsingham in Norfolk became a holy site of pilgrimage after visions of the Virgin Mary had been seen there. The great cathedral city of Cologne was another centre of pilgrimage, as was Compostela; further afield, many pilgrims made the long journey to Jerusalem, available for visits from Christian pilgrims after the Emperor Frederick II had negotiated peace with the 'infidels', and had himself crowned king of the holy city.

Pilgrims (travelling in groups for companionship and safety) would travel to shrines in their own country and abroad to celebrate their devotion to the church, to seek pardon for their sins and to ask favours of the saint whose relics were preserved in that place. The traditional image of a pilgrim is of one who travels humbly and simply, dressed in plain clothes, often on foot, carrying a staff. The emblem of a pilgrim is the scallop or cockle shell, worn on cap or hood. This was particularly the symbol of St James, patron saint of military crusaders, and the journey to his shrine in Compostela, northern Spain, was, and still is, one of the great pilgrim routes across Europe. The shells may originally have been real ones, but were later moulded in lead, as were most other pilgrim badges.

By the time Chaucer decided to use a group of pilgrims as a framework for his *Canterbury Tales*, reasons for pilgrimage had become less exclusively devotional. By the fourteenth century it had also certainly become a profitable business for enterprising people, as well as a popular pastime. The tourist industry began to take off. The Venetians offered a regular ferry service carrying travellers to and from the Holy Land. The monks of Cluny, the greatest religious house in France, ran a string of hostels along the entire route between their monastery and Compostela. Many travel guides were produced, giving information about accommodation available along the route. One for Compostela contained useful Basque vocabulary, and a description of what to see in the cathedral. Horse dealers did a healthy trade hiring out horses to pilgrims.

There was great competition for popular relics between the religious establishments, which sometimes led to rather obvious forgeries. At least two places, for instance, claimed to possess the head of John the Baptist. Pilgrims began to bring home their own souvenirs, and to house them in their local churches, like the fourteenth century traveller William Wey, who proudly deposited in his Wiltshire village church his maps, a reproduction of St Veronica's handkerchief, which he had rubbed on the pillars of 'the tempyl of Jerusalem', and a large number of stones picked up in sites around the Holy Land. His parish priest was presumably delighted. Badges and emblems made of lead were sold at shrines, and eagerly purchased as souvenirs by travellers – the cockle shell for St James, the palm tree from Jericho. At Canterbury it was possible to buy an assortment of badges – an image of the head of the saint, St Thomas, riding a horse, or a little bell, or a small ampulla [bottle] to hold sacred water. Permission was given from Rome for the local religious houses to obtain a licence to manufacture these.

Some of Chaucer's pilgrims seem to have genuinely devout reasons for visiting Canterbury: the Knight, for instance, has come straight from his military expeditions abroad, fighting for Christendom, and his simple coat is still stained from its contact with his coat of mail. On the other hand, the Wife of Bath, although an enthusiastic pilgrim, hardly seems to be travelling in a spirit of piety or devotion. She lists the places she has visited like a seasoned traveller determined to visit as many tourist attractions as possible. Nevertheless she, like all the others, is travelling in search of something. By using a pilgrimage as the frame on which to hang his stories and characterisations, Chaucer was able to point out the way in which attitudes and standards were changing and old values were being lost.

Geoffrey Chaucer

Geoffrey Chaucer

BIOGRAPHICAL NOTES

1340?   The actual date of his birth is uncertain, but he was near 60 when he died. His father and grandfather were both vintners – wealthy London merchants, who supplied wines to the king's court.

Chaucer was introduced to court life in his teens. By the age of 16 he was employed in the service of the wife of the king's son, Lionel, later Duke of Clarence.

1359   He fought in France in the army of Edward III. He was captured and imprisoned, but released on payment of his ransom by the duke.

Chaucer was clearly valued by the king himself and other members of the powerful royal family. In the **1360s** and **1370s** he was sent abroad on diplomatic missions to France, Genoa, Florence and Lombardy.

1360s   He married Philippa de Roet, a maid-in-waiting to Edward III's wife, Queen Philippa. His wife's half-sister was Katherine Swynford, third wife of John of Gaunt. The link with this powerful Duke of Lancaster was an important one; the duke was Chaucer's patron, who in later life gave Chaucer a pension of £10 a year.

1368   Chaucer wrote *The Book of the Duchess*, a poem on the death of Duchess Blanche, first wife of John of Gaunt.

1374   The position of Comptroller of Customs for the port of London was given to Chaucer, and in the same year the king granted him a pitcher of wine daily. Other lucrative administrative posts became his later.

1374–84   Chaucer began his unfinished work *The House of Fame*, and wrote *The Parlement of Fowles* – possibly for the marriage of Richard II.

1386   Like the Franklin in *The Canterbury Tales*, Chaucer was appointed 'Knight of the Shire' or Parliamentary representative for Kent.

Early 1380s He wrote *Troilus and Criseyde*.

It seems that, in spite of the royal and noble patronage he enjoyed, Chaucer was an extravagant man, and money slipped through his fingers. In 1389 he was appointed Clerk of the King's Works by Richard II, but the position lasted only two years. It may be that the poet lost his official position and favour during the political upheavals of Richard's reign. Richard later gave him a pension of £20 for life, which Chaucer frequently asked for 'in advance'. Threats of arrest for non-payment of debts were warded off by letters of protection from the crown.

1388   Chaucer probably began to formulate his ideas for *The Canterbury Tales* at this time – perhaps after making a pilgrimage himself.

1391   He was appointed deputy forester for Petherton, Somerset (an administrative post) and may have spent some time there.

1399   Henry IV, son of John of Gaunt, became king, and Chaucer was
           awarded a new pension of 40 marks (about £26), which allowed him
           to live his few remaining months in comfort.

1400   Chaucer died in October and was buried in Westminster Abbey –
           acknowledged as the greatest English poet of his age.

CHAUCER THE WRITER AND SCHOLAR

Although actively involved in diplomatic life, moving in court circles and travelling
extensively, Chaucer was also an extremely well-read man. His own works show the
influence of both classical writers and more recent French and Italian works. The
wide range of biblical, classical and contemporary literary references in the Wife of
Bath's Prologue and Tale bear witness to his learning, and he confesses to owning 60
books – a considerable library in those days. Many ideas and themes which occur in
The Canterbury Tales have been adapted from the works of classical and
contemporary sources known to Chaucer and to at least some of his audiences.

Some of his best known works have been mentioned above. His earliest works,
such as *The Book of the Duchess*, show the influence of courtly and allegorical French
love poetry, in particular the *Roman de la Rose*. Chaucer's work is a dream-poem in
this tradition, but also a lament for lost love, written after the death of the beautiful
Blanche of Lancaster, John of Gaunt's first wife.

The House of Fame, an unfinished narrative poem, suggests both French and Italian
influences. Chaucer is almost the only writer of the century outside Italy to show
knowledge of Dante (1265–1321), and uses this poem to challenge Dante's claim
that it is possible to know the truth about people's behaviour and motives in the
past. He also admired the writings of two other Italians, Petrarch and Boccaccio, and
may have met Boccaccio whilst on diplomatic business in Italy. In fact, Boccaccio's
Decameron, written forty years or so before *The Canterbury Tales*, employs the
linking device (in his case a group of sophisticated men and women, entertaining
one another with storytelling in a country retreat, whilst the Black Death rages in
Florence) that Chaucer was to use later with far greater subtlety, variety and skill.

In both *Troilus and Criseyde*, his moving re-telling of the tale of love and betrayal at
the time of the Trojan War, and in *The Canterbury Tales* Chaucer shows the debt he
owed to classical writers like Homer, Horace, Virgil, Ovid and Plato, as well as
thorough knowledge of biblical writings from the Old and New Testaments and the
Apocrypha. He knew the writings of many theologians respected in the Middle
Ages, such as St Jerome and St Augustine. He greatly admired the Roman
philosopher Boethius, and translated his work *De Consolatione Philosophiae* from the
Latin original into English. His writings showed an interest in astronomy and
astrology (the Franklin's Tale reveals a considerable amount of detailed knowledge in
this area) and he wrote *A Treatise on the Astrolabe*, explaining the workings of this
astronomical instrument, which he dedicated to 'little Lewise' – presumably his
young son, who died in childhood. We hear nothing of him later.

These are just some of the best known of Chaucer's own writings; they give some
idea of the breadth and depth of his scholarship and interests.

Town v. gown: life in Oxford in the fourteenth century

Lively and unruly young men dominate the early stories in *The Canterbury Tales*: love for Emily results in ceaseless battle and pointless death in the Knight's Tale; the Reeve's Tale features two enterprising Cambridge students; and the unfinished Cook's Tale is set in London, where a pleasure-seeking young apprentice spends most of his time dancing, drinking, betting and philandering. Chaucer chooses to set the Miller's Tale in fourteenth-century Oxford, a busy small town, dominated then, as now, by its large student population.

Although students were supposedly training to become churchmen, by the 1380s many were taking up positions outside the church – as lawyers, administrators, members of the growing civil service. At the beginning of the century all education had been linked to religious houses, and controlled by the Catholic church, but the Black Death of 1348, with its subsequent reappearances in the 1360s, had resulted in huge losses amongst clergy. There was concern that educational establishments needed to be encouraged, even those not necessarily linked to the church. Winchester, the first school designed to educate boys not necessarily intending to become churchmen, was established by William of Wykeham in 1382. Likely students went on to the universities of Oxford and Cambridge, some as young as 14, where they would be taught the basic disciplines of medieval education: Grammar, Logic, Rhetoric, Geometry, Arithmetic, Music and Astronomy. Some lived in the colleges, but these were usually students intending to go on to become clerics. Many, like Nicholas, lodged in rooms provided by townsmen. They relied for financial support on their friends and family. Nicholas' small library and comfortable room suggest that he was generously maintained.

The principal towns of England – London (by far the largest), Bristol, York and the university towns of Oxford and Cambridge – were lively places. Many of the houses were also shops, with the living quarters over the business. There were bakers, brewers, butchers, fishmongers, blacksmiths, wheelwrights, carpenters, builders, stonemasons, merchants selling silks, cloth, shoes, jewellery; doctors, alchemists, fortune tellers, pubs, markets selling fresh produce, street entertainers, fast food outlets, musicians, guildhalls for various trades, and plenty of churches. Many of the wealthier residents had sizeable kitchen gardens, with fruit and vegetable plots, and probably room for a pig and some chickens. Townsfolk were not cut off from the surrounding countryside. Produce from outlying farms was sold in the markets of the nearest towns and villages. Craftsmen such as John the carpenter were commissioned to work on outlying estates. Millers provided their services for all the farmers of the area. In the Reeve's Tale the miller in the Cambridgeshire village of Trumpington ground corn for the university colleges.

Although student lodgers provided a source of extra income for their landlords, they were not always popular with the townspeople of Oxford or Cambridge. There are numerous reports of riots and disturbances between town and gown. Some students worked hard at their studies, but many were dissolute and idle. As 'clerks' they were exempt from the justice meted out by local courts, and answerable only to church courts. In 1355 a dispute between an Oxford tavern keeper and a group of students, over an unpaid bill, resulted in students setting fire to the inn, and, ultimately, large parts of the town. As a result the townspeople turned against them; 63 students were killed, and the university was temporarily closed down, until the king intervened. An annual fine was paid thereafter by 63 burghers of the town of Oxford to the vice-chancellor of the university – a practice which continued for 500 years. Chaucer's original audience would remember this well, particularly since, as recently as 1381, a riot between townspeople and members of Cambridge university had resulted in the burning of all that institution's records.

In the Miller's Tale, therefore, the young student would need to tread warily around his wealthy landlord if he wished to enjoy his wife without fear of reprisals. Four of the five fabliaux in *The Canterbury Tales* deal with clever young men outwitting old, dull husbands. Flaunting superior knowledge, and using wit and intelligence to outsmart John, Nicholas represents all that townsfolk distrusted and disliked in the student population.

Not all students were like Nicholas: compare him with the 'Clerke of Oxenforde' depicted in the General Prologue (see pages 38–9 of the Cambridge School Chaucer edition).

Merton College, founded in 1264, was the centre in England for mathematical, scientific and astronomical study, and Chaucer's description of Nicholas' skills links him with this location.

Merton College Library –
then as now

Astronomy and astrology

Chaucer was interested in and knowledgeable about astronomy. He wrote a treatise on the use of the astrolabe for navigational purposes; by giving Nicholas an astrolabe as well as his own copy of Ptolemy's definitive astronomical work, the *Almageste*, he suggests that the young clerk is not totally a fraud – he does indeed know something about the study of astronomy, considered to be one of the most prestigious and challenging branches of knowledge in the medieval world, and one for which Merton College, Oxford was famous throughout Europe.

By the fourteenth century there was increased awareness among scientists of the movements of planets, and the way in which sun and moon affected the weather and the movements of tides. As scientists discovered more about the regular and irregular movement of heavenly bodies they began to realise how much there was still to learn about the vastness of the universe and its structure. True astronomers dismissed 'fortune-telling' and magic, though they certainly believed that study of the movement of planets could enable them to predict global and personal events. Some astrologers could well be called magicians or charlatans, and were more concerned with attempting to foretell men's futures by studying the heavens. The idea that a man's behaviour and actions were influenced by the position of the planets at the time and place of his birth was fundamental to much medieval thinking. Simple men, like John the carpenter, would confuse Nicholas' knowledge of astronomy with magical arts – a confusion the young clerk exploits to his own advantage.

Religion and its place in everyday society

Oxford, like every other town and village in England, was dominated by the influence of the church. Everyone was expected to attend regular services, make confessions and give offerings. The church ceremonies, brightly coloured wall paintings and music provided most people's only artistic experiences, together with dramatic sermons (often preached by travelling friars) and the popular mystery plays, performed by the local guilds. Hospitals were run by monastic orders. All education, including, of course, the university itself, was in the hands of clerics. The students, as well as their masters, were originally expected to become priests. The church was also a wealthy landowner, and an employer of labour. Lay workers were required, for instance, on farms, in woodland, dairies and kitchens, like John the carpenter, who regularly works at the outlying church estate at Osney. The church had extensive influence over the population, not just spiritually, but over wages, housing, and food supplies.

Religious observance was part of the background of everyday life: the church bells, summoning monks and clergy to the various church services such as lauds, vespers or matins would mark off the hours throughout every day; ordinary people automatically called on saints for help in times of disaster. In the Miller's Tale, for instance, these are local saints, such as St Neot and St Frideswide, as well as the more widely known St Benedict and St Peter. Not only do the clerks have an obvious familiarity with prayers, church services and bible stories: Alison visits the church for a service specifically for women; she and her husband both recite the Lord's Prayer, and the story of Noah from the Old Testament is clearly well known.

It is quite clear from the Miller's Tale that the plays known to us as 'mystery' plays figured largely in the religious awareness of common people. These plays, still performed today in town such as York and Chester, were enacted by ordinary townspeople. Plays, depicting particular biblical incidents, were allotted to various guilds or groups of tradespeople, and were often appropriate to their skill or 'mystery'. Shipwrights, or sometimes carpenters, might perform the building of Noah's ark, and the story of Herod and the slaughter of the innocents was a particularly suitable choice for the barbers (Absolon, therefore, as a part-time barber [see line 218] would obviously have the opportunity to play Herod). The plays were usually performed in May or June, around the time of the feast of Corpus Christi. A procession of carts, each one used as a stage on wheels, would travel through the town, each wagon stopping at selected locations to perform the play to watching crowds in the street, before moving on to the next location. They provided an important way of conveying bible stories to a largely illiterate audience in an entertaining and exciting way. Most ordinary people, like John and Alison, would be very familiar with what they portrayed.

Nevertheless, it seems that for some at least this religious observance was often just lip service. By the late fourteenth century satirical comments about the greed, lecherousness and ungodly behaviour of churchmen were common in literature of the time. Chaucer's jokes about the Monk, Friar, and Prioress – even the Summoner and Pardoner – were tame compared to some of the savage criticism that came their way from other writers. In the Miller's Tale we are shown that churchgoing was an accepted routine, but not necessarily undertaken in a way that was spiritually satisfying: neither Alison nor Absolon seems to be thinking about God during the church services. And although Nicholas and Absolon both clearly know their bible well, neither of them uses his knowledge with any religious intent. As for John the carpenter – he might be seen to be the most affected by an awareness of divine power, but his understanding of biblical matters seems decidedly flawed, and his feverish prayers seem like a superstitious gabble rather than an indication of faith in God's mercy. He regards the divine mystery of God's purpose regarding humanity as something best ignored by ordinary men. He, and the Miller himself, seem to find it as perplexing as understanding women.

Chaucer warned his audience from the start that the Miller's Tale would be a 'cherles tale' – a fabliau – in which moral judgements would have no place. Alison and her two clerks are concerned only with their own pleasure, they feel no sense of guilt or sin. Only the clever and the lucky escape punishment, and the world laughs heartlessly at the rest. But punishment and laughter are totally related to this world, not the next; and Chaucer is at pains to point out, as the pilgrim narrators of *The Canterbury Tales* proceed towards their destination, that this is only one way of looking at life.

Longer questions on the Miller's Tale

1 THE WAY THE TALE IS TOLD
   a) How effectively does the language and narrative style of this tale reflect its form (the fabliau) and its teller?
   b) How important are the five senses (touch, taste, sight, sound and smell) in the telling of this tale?
   c) Although the tale has been 'given' to the Miller by Chaucer, does the way it is narrated really sound as if it is being told by an uneducated person?
   d) Chaucer describes people and places with great vividness, creating powerful visual images. Choose one or two examples of descriptive passages and analyse the way in which they achieve their power, and their importance in the tale as a whole.
   e) How far does the Prologue (lines 1–78) lay the foundations for the tale itself?

2 HUMOUR
   a) What variety of humour do you find in this tale? Is it satirical? Bawdy? Full of absurd situations? Is it too distasteful, unfeeling or vulgar to appeal to a modern audience? Does its strength lie not so much in what happens as the way it is told? Choose one or two sections that you particularly enjoyed, and analyse their appeal.
   b) How skilfully does Chaucer use dialogue in telling this tale? Choose a section containing more than one voice and prepare a reading, showing how character and humour are revealed.

3 APPEARANCE AND REALITY
   a) How frequently, and to what effect, does Chaucer use imagery derived from the natural world in this tale?
   b) Do we obtain a clearer idea of characters from what we are told about them, or from what they do and say? Discuss the contrast between appearance and reality in relation to two of the four main characters.
   c) What happens in this tale to courtly ideas of the pining lover and the inaccessible lady?
   d) How crucial to the tale are the fantasies created by both Absolon and Nicholas?

4 CHAUCER AND THE FOURTEENTH CENTURY
   a) How vividly, and by what means, does Chaucer give us a sense of life in medieval Oxford?
   b) What deductions can you draw about marriage, the role of women and relationships between the sexes from this tale?
   c) How much do we learn about religion and attitudes to it?

Glossary of frequently used words

amended	improve	**noot**	don't know
anon	immediately, at once	**oon**	one
axed	asked	**ooth/othes**	oath/oaths
bad	told, advised	**pardee**	by God
bigile	deceive	**prively**	secretly
cleped/ycleped	called, named	**quite**	pay back
clerk	educated man	**sely**	foolish, innocent
eek	also	**seye/seyn**	speak, mean, tell
gan	began	**shilde**	forbid
gentillesse	courtesy, good manners	**sholde**	should, would
gnof	lout, uncultured person	**sikerly**	certainly, truly
		siketh	sigh/sighed
hende	nice, personable	**swich**	such
ilk/ilke	this same	**swinke**	toil, labour, work
koude	knew	**swoote**	sweet, sweet-smelling
laudes	first hour of church day	**thanne**	then
		thilke	this, that
		trouthe	pledge, promise
lemman	sweetheart, lover	**wende**	thought, believed
maad	made	**whilom**	once upon a time
namely	particularly	**wiste**	knew
namoore	no more	**wood**	mad
nolde [ne wolde]	would not		